Why is the book important?

We are driven today by an insatiable need for self-realization through accumulation of things, acknowledgment of self, and exercise of power. A change is called for in the way we go about the business of living. There is a need for a radical change in this approach to life in interpersonal relations such as family, society, government and even the church. The crucial question is, "What change is needed as we move along on our journey, view and react to the landscape?"

The title of this book, *Hope Realized*, inspires us to believe that our life's journey can have a positive outcome. We can claim a vision for our life and live with the hope that we can realize that vision. Such a belief enables us to endure the hardships and difficulties, overcome the hurdles and realize our purpose for living. Such a movement requires turning away from merely living for self-gain, affirming the holy/eternal presence and becoming a person of sensitivity toward others.

How is the book purchased?

You may purchase Hope Realized from Sam Laine, 275 Home Place, Collierville, TN, 38017. Send a check to him for $18.50. along with your mailing address.

earlier effort. I was encouraged by my wife and others to share these articles with others.

What would occur if in the give-and-take of life we approach a problem, an issue, a dysfunctional relationship, a social group, the activities of government or any other institution by asking questions that recognize the blessings and opportunities for new life available to us? We learn that each point in time becomes the realization of hope because of our daily blessings and future possibilities.

What is the book about?

The book is about living a hopeful life! When I first decided to publish these articles, I was going to share them as they were chronologically written. However, the more I studied them, the more I became aware of a fundamental perspective that was used to create them. Therefore, I have tried to capture this perspective in four interlocking themes with an overarching motif of "Hope Realized". Life is a journey (Journey Along the Way) where we then (View the Landscape). This journey is one of self-realization. Interestingly, the beginning place throughout the articles was not with myself, but by way of a caring interest in and response to others (Affirm Others/Realize Self). Then I found a captivating thought that energizes this human process (Acknowledge an Eternal/Holy Presence). You will find that the articles are organized chronologically under these themes.

The people of the world today seem to be in a dynamic struggle for self-realization. I truly believe we are living in a time of significant change and meaning; I would call it Karros time, time of meaning, where a dramatic shift is happening. The prominent stress on self-realization in our society today is primarily on the development of our selves through achievement and acquisition. This notion is challenged at its roots. Instead of living as individuals in a social unit, we are called to live together as persons in community. Instead of being primarily focused on ourselves, we must first affirm the existence of others as we seek self-realization.

Life is more than a journey from birth to death. There is a holy/eternal presence calling us out of ourselves to interact with others, nature, the universe and the holy/eternal presence that gives our journey shape and meaning. Hope sustains us along the way and clarifies our vision for the living of each day. Hope is realized!

HOW TO READ HOPE REALIZED

Hope Realized developed out of the though process of the author. It began with one hundred and fifty essays written over a three and a half year period. By analyzing the essays a pattern of thinking emerged. The essays are organized around four major themes that develop the title, Hope Realized. The Preface will lead you through the underlying though processes that created the essays. The Introduction to the entire book provides the insight that will enable an understanding of the four interlocking themes. Each theme has an introduction that should provide a context in which the related essays can be read with enriched understanding. Then finally the epilog is the author's attempt to write a word of defining insight.

How does one read this book? The essays provide the flesh for the essential word about the style of "self-realization" that gives hope and sanity for the living of these days. But the essays need to be read after the reader claims an understanding of the heart beat of the book. The author suggest that to claim the heart beat of Hope Realized read the Preface, the General Introduction, the Introductions to each theme and finally the Epilog before ever reading the first essay. Then read the essays, at random or in order, in the light of the related introduction. The essays for some have become spiritual food for the enrichment of daily living. Hope Realized has a heart that beats with a beckoning rhythm. The author provide the Last Word that gives insight into whom he considers to be the one who gives shape, inspiration , passion and guidance to his life!

Questions People Are Asking

Why did you write the book?
I wrote the book to help people realize hope along their human journey. After nearly eighty years of living, over two thousand sermons, and an equal number of articles in the church newsletter, I entertained the notion that surely there is a collection of thought that could be shared. I have been serving in my retirement as part-time pastor in a small church in Oakland (Fayette County), Tennessee. Several years ago, I approached the owner of one of the county's weekly newspapers with the idea of writing an article each week. It was a good notion and he was willing to give me the opportunity. My intention was to reach out into the county with insights that might be useful for daily living. So actually the book is the outcome this

A new dimension
in devotional guides

Hope
Realized

BLESSINGS AND OPPORTUNITIES
PROVIDE PATHWAYS TO A HOPEFUL
PRESENT AND FUTURE

"This is my *Father's World* and to
my *listening* ears, all *nature* sings and
round me sing the music of the *spheres.*
This is my *Father's World* and though
the wrong seems oft so *strong,*
God is the ruler yet." Maltbie Babcock

BY SAM B. LAINE

"Yes, hope can be *realized!* Hope is a better
day, a *fuller* life, a *brighter* tomorrow can be
realized. Go tell it on the *mountain* that
hope can be realized." SBL

A fresh look at self realization
that restores sanity to our world.

Photos taken by Sam B. Laine
David Yawn, Editor
Jocelyn Regenwether, Proofer
Lynn Parrish, Designer

First American Edition
ISBN 978-0-615-71563-6

Lighthouse Leadership Series Imprint

This book is dedicated to Becky, my wife,
who has shown me abounding love, devotion
and encouragement throughout our
nearly sixty years of marriage.

Table of Contents

Preface

I have arrived at the conclusion that after nearly eighty years of living, over two thousand sermons, and an equal number of articles in the church newsletter, that surely there is a collection of thought that could be shared. I had been serving as part-time pastor in a small church in Oakland (Fayette County), Tennessee. Several years ago, I approached Butch Ray, the owner of the Fayette Falcon, a weekly newspaper, with the idea of writing an article each week. It was a good notion and he was willing to give me the opportunity. I sought to reach out into the county with thoughts that might be useful for daily living.

There were several ministers who already were writing articles using scripture as their source of inspiration. My intention was somewhat different. I wanted these articles to become what I call "lessons in living" that emerge out of the depths of my own journey and life experiences and observations. In free association, I focused on an idea, an experience or a happening. The thoughts that surfaced became the resources for the articles. My accumulation of knowledge and personal experiences became the incubator for the birth of these articles. In this preface, I want to share with you what I think served as the catalyst for shaping and organizing these thoughts.

I asked several people to read these articles to determine their usefulness for the general public. Before I go any further, I want to express my gratitude to Stephanie Wall, a good friend and fellow faith traveler; Laine Halfacre, my grandson; and Warner Davis, a fellow minister who encouraged me in pursuing this publication. My wife, Becky, has been at the forefront suggesting that I bring these articles together in a book.

One of the readers suggested that I had captured the underlying theme in the first article. In that article, I talked about seeing life through the half empty or half full side of an hourglass. I pointed out that we, as humans, have a tendency to look at life through the half-empty side. We focus on the losses and failures in life. And with such a focus, we create a negative and almost impossible reality with which to move through life.

When we can take the half-full side of the hourglass and deal with the various aspects of life, the outcome is quite different. This means seeking to develop our life in terms of the blessings for a happy life and the opportunities for a fresh start that are available to us. And with this focus, we then create a reality where we become possibility thinkers and doers. It's like moving from, "No, I can't do it" to "Yes, I can do it." It's like migrating from "No, it won't happen" to "Yes, it will happen."

What would occur if, in the give-and-take of life, we approach a problem, an issue, a dysfunctional relationship, a social group, the activities of government or any other institution by asking questions that emphasize the blessings and opportunities for new life available to us? Once we recognize the blessings and opportunities, we would proceed to consider how we might build on what we discover.

When I suggested to my editor, David Yawn, that I was thinking about entitling this book, *Half Full ~ Half Empty*, he encouraged me to think about another title, *Hope Realized*. Dr. Martin Luther King is known for many thoughtful and eloquent phrases; the one most notably is "Keep Hope Alive!" President Obama has written a book entitled, *The Audacity of Hope*. I am reminded of the angels at the birth of the Christ child; included in their words were: "the hopes and fears of all the years are met in thee tonight." Hope is the fuel that keeps us on the go when everything is crumbling around us.

When Dr. King spoke boldly to "keep hope alive" he was saying, "Keep the fuel of hope in your spiritual tank, so you can keep on keeping on in spite of IT (whatever IT may be)." The aforementioned book title, *The Audacity of Hope*, causes us to think it is almost presumptuous to believe that all will indeed be well.

I think we need to ask the question, What is hope? *"Hope is the emotional state, the opposite of which is despair, which promotes the belief in a positive outcome related to events and happenings in one's life."* [the free encyclopedia] I think the title *Hope Realized* is on target. When you look at the half-full side of the hour glass and focus on the blessings and opportunities, hope can be truly realized. I am inviting you to read these articles with the awareness that hope can be realized in the most dubious of circumstances. How? By finding that blessing or opportunity that frees and empowers us to press on to claim that new day, that new life, and, yes, that fresh start.

For blessings and opportunities to serve as a catalyst for this fresh start, life needs to have a purpose. I am reminded of a thought my mother planted in my mind. She would say, "Sam, God has a plan and a purpose for your life." As years give way to years and we are able to look through the rearview mirror at where we've been, we see how the purpose of our life is still unfolding. With such a rear view we are able, hopefully, to claim the future.

Each step along the way becomes a place, an event, a revelation in time that enables us to live out the present and to look to the future with hope. As we have taken advantage of the blessings and opportunities along the journey, we have begun to catch a glimpse of our future. Each point in time becomes the realization of hope because of the possibilities of the future.

When I retired, I created a motto that somewhat defines the way I look at life; this saying is "Future Grasp." This phrase brings into focus my introduction to these articles with words from the writings of Robert Browning. In the poem, "Rabbi Ben Ezra," Browning penned these words:

> *"Grow old along with me, the best is yet to be;*
> *The last for which the first was meant."*

Introduction

When I first decided to publish these articles, I was going to share them as they were chronologically written. However, the more I studied them, the more I became aware of a fundamental perspective that was used to create them. Therefore, I have tried to capture this perspective in four interlocking themes. Life is a journey (Journey Along the Way) where we then (View the Landscape). This journey is one of self-realization. Interestingly, I found that the beginning place throughout the articles was not with myself, but by way of a caring interest in and response to others (Affirm Others/Realize Self). Then I found a captivating thought that energizes this human process (Acknowledge an Eternal/Holy Presence).

I have organized the articles chronologically under these themes. Each chapter has an introduction to the theme. The people of the world today seem to be in a dynamic struggle for self-realization. I truly believe we are living in a time of significant change and meaning; I would call it Karros time, a time of meaning, where a dramatic shift is happening. I want to let the preface assist us as we seek to deal with these shifting plates in time. I think as you read this introduction you will find an order and movement to the material where the parts and the whole provide a cohesive and meaningful journey.

Life is a journey from birth to death. And for hope to be realized, fear has to be overcome along the way for it immobilizes us. We can't remain in place but must reach beyond the common and ordinary and embrace the eternal. In order to do this, a guiding purpose is claimed to keep us on track. The title of the first chapter is "Along the Way."

As we move Along the Way, our lives take shape by Viewing the Landscape. We come to understand that endurance is needed for us to keep pressing on. We look at what is happening around us and to us through the scope of a hopeful purpose; we do this to claim the opportunities for engagement along the way. This enables reaching beyond the present where we grasp the future and realize the fulfillment of our hopeful purpose. The other focus is to be aware of the blessings that have enriched our lives and given encouragement to us to continue the journey. The title to the second chapter is "View the Landscape" by maintaining endurance, claiming our opportunities and rejoicing in our blessings. This allows us as persons to put to death despair and disappointment; and proceed with the possibility of hope realized.

As I have written, much of the human effort along the journey takes shape around self-realization. The prominent stress on self-realization in our society today is primarily on the development of ourselves through achievement and acquisition. The third chapter describes how this notion is challenged at its roots. Instead of living as individuals in a social unit, we are called to live together as people in community. Instead of being primarily focused on ourselves, we must first affirm the existence of others as we seek self-realization.

We, individually, are not the center of creation, but together with others and all creation are the completion of creation. The title of the third chapter suggests that as we "Affirm Others/(we)Realize Self," then hope is realized as a blessing for all the peoples of the world.

The last chapter, "Acknowledge a Holy/Eternal Presence" seeks to remind us of the expanding nature of life and the existence of an eternal/spiritual reality. Without acknowledging the holy/eternal presence, life is encapsulated in time and hope is like a broken limb, hard to hold onto for support and never realized. But it is more than a journey from birth to death; there is a holy/eternal presence calling us out of ourselves to interact with others, nature, the universe and the holy/eternal presence that gives it shape and meaning. Hope sustains us along the way and clarifies our vision for the living of each day. Hope is realized!

1. Journey Along the Way

My wife and I have developed a vital interest in taking trips near and far. As I organize my articles for publication, even now I am preparing a trip to the Grand Tetons, Yellowstone National Park and Mt. Rushmore. We will drive over 1,600 miles to reach our destination. As we move across the country, there will be much to see and do. Of course, we must keep our eyes on the road so we get there safely. Yet, a failure to observe the landscape will deprive us of much. Life's journey is similar; we should not be so preoccupied with reaching our goal that we fail to stop and engage what we see and hear. We need to appreciate the sights and sounds and interact with the people we encounter.

As I have *moved along the way*, I have come to recognize certain practices or ways of looking at life that are useful. Creativity and maintenance are required. Be sure you have something to do to encourage you. Be sure you have people with whom to share your life to enrich you. Be sure you have places to go to expand your horizon.

I enjoy travelling because each trip brings new insights. This travel not only broadens my horizon, but helps me understand the importance of other people, their visions, their struggles and my opportunity to respond to others. We should take time to stop and celebrate the beauty of life and be sensitive to the struggles and accomplishments of others. Be careful, though, never to stay forever in one place or forever embrace one notion or personal opinion as absolute; you then may lose the beauty and value you have gained. As we move to new places, explore new ideas and engage new relationships, we find that touch of eternity is at least in our grasp.

How often have we heard that life is a journey from birth to death? *Fear of death* has a way of choking our daily life and dismantling the appearance of eternity. The clouds of death can hover over us with a foreboding presence as we move along the way. Unless we are adequately prepared, the fear of death will <u>control</u> the way we live. I believe that this fear is noted in the feeling that we may cease being; our life seems to be like a puff of smoke that fades away. So it becomes necessary to have a purpose for living that is shaped by a hopeful tomorrow.

My belief in Jesus Christ gives me a life that has this eternal dimension that sets me free from the fear of death. I also believe that a person, by exploring one's inner self can be in touch with this sense of the Eternal, for all persons are made in the image of God. When we are able to expand our life beyond the stars and the moon, we heighten our senses and interests, and engage the eternal, the fear of death will no longer control our daily life. This is embodied in the admonition "to seek first the kingdom of God and God's righteousness and all other things will be given you." (Matthew 6:33, 34)

We do not claim eternity by living as settlers, but as pilgrims. This calls for reaching for the uncommon and extraordinary. Life can be described as moving away from one moment in time and progression toward another. At any point along the way, there is the temptation to look for our security in established ways. We must not yield to such a temptation, rather always reach for the stars; yes, accept the challenges to go beyond where we have already been.

Learning the art of communication is essential to the ability to explore new horizons. Listen to the new sounds in the wind. Speak as if you have heard a fresh voice. More often than not, people choose to establish their security in making absolute what they believe or making holy the place where they have settled. The challenge is to claim our freedom by taking the longer view and the unchartered road.

This expansion of life from time into eternity just doesn't automatically happen. It requires preparation each day so that tomorrow is new and significant. But along the way, we accumulate unnecessary baggage. In several of the articles in this chapter, there are descriptions of what is needed for a person to take the longer view. I learned from spring gardening of the need to weed the flowerbeds before planting; this is the same with life. Just like the weeds in the soil, we have to remove those things of little value in us. Another way of saying this is to remove the psychic pus to achieve the virtuous life. Everybody can't be number one, but everybody can be a winner.

We learn that, at a certain point in our journey from birth to death, the growth process changes into a death process. As I have said, it takes a purpose, a reason for living, to sustain our life in the face of the death factor. I often tell folks that I am a young man in an old man's body. I am reminded of the words of the Apostle Paul, in which he says, "While our bodies are growing old, there is a new person being born anew within us." [Paraphrase] In order for that new person to come to life, we have to claim the purpose for our existence. As I have mentioned elsewhere, when I was a child, I was required to learn the Children's Catechism. There was the question, "What is a person's chief end?" The answer was "To glorify God and enjoy him forever." Beyond this overarching purpose, each of us has to find our unique reason for living. We will then realize that *goodness* can become the true chord played on the instrument of life.

Grand Tetons, Wyoming

"We should not be so **preoccupied** with reaching our **goals** in life that we fail to **stop** and **engage** what we **see** and **hear**. We need to **appreciate** the **sights** and **sounds** and **interact** with the **people** we encounter." SBL

Hawaii

Beijing, China

Cambodia

The Wailing Wall, Jerusalem

Zambia, Africa

"We *individually* are not the **center** of *creation*, but **together** with *others* and all *creation* are the **completion** of *creation*." SBL

New York City

Vietnam

Purposeful Living

FEBRUARY, 18. 2008

I would like to come into your homes with a story about two members of a church that I served many years ago. Both of these men lost their wives by death. The journeys taken by these men were quite different. It would be easier to tell the story by giving these gentlemen names, Roy and Bill.

Roy has a sense of the providence of God in his life. He also had interests outside of his normal routine of living. He took pictures of wild flowers. He decided to take his many pictures, which in those days were slides, and create a slide presentation using Psalms from the Bible as background readings. He took his presentations, and by invitation, shared this inspirational program with others.

Bill, who had a drinking problem in his earlier years, became caught up in his grief and loneliness. Bill drank more and more; he became increasingly depressed.

Roy seemed to be more aware of God's providential presence in his life. He concluded that God has a continuing purpose for his life. This may seem pretty simple, but Roy found a sense of purpose in sharing the beauty of his photography and the richness of the Psalms. Bill seemed to lose whatever purpose for living he might have had.

This story shows that our ability to continue our life's journey depends on our believing that we do have a purpose for living. This purpose is beyond the usual and ordinary routine. I guess I acquired this belief from my mother who said to me early in life, "Sam, God has a plan and purpose for you." This belief has given me the vehicle to ride well into the future.

A little over seven years ago, I had bypass surgery. Several years prior to this surgery, I had a cardiac arrest and nearly died. These two experiences empowered the belief that "God has a plan and purpose for my life" and put my feet on new ground. As we grow older, sometimes we are prone to become resigned to the ordinary and routine aspects of life. We often live to maintain our health and engage in activities merely to enjoy the passing of the days. Well, I believe that life is more than "let's eat, drink and be merry, for tomorrow we may die." I have a license plate on the front of my car, on which you will find the words "love and justice". Both of these words mean living life outside ourselves for the well-being of others. My faith in Jesus Christ motivates me to find the fullness of life in the opportunities of love and justice. Try each day to respond to the opportunities for love and justice around you. You won't regret it!

Freedom from Death

MARCH 18, 2008

Next Sunday, all over the world Christians will be gathering to worship the risen Christ. The common theme will be that Jesus "died and was raised from the dead to set us free from sin and death." I believe that the declarations of the Christian Church spend much more time on "freedom from sin." I want to take time with you this week to reflect on the far-reaching meaning of freedom from death.

When I was about nine years old, I came down from my upstairs bedroom and stood outside of the kitchen where my mother and father were. I had just had what some might call a nightmare. I was overwhelmed with the notion that I would die someday and would never be again. This sense of not being is a frightening experience. Faith in Jesus Christ is supposed to bring us close to God who is loving and forgiving. With this sense of closeness, we are encouraged to believe that we have a life that will never die. With such a belief we are able to overcome this horrible fear of not being someday. The belief that Jesus has been raised gives us the hope that when we die, we too will be raised from the dead.

But there is a profound meaning of this victory over death for our day-to-day living. I don't know if you realize it, death has a choking effect on our daily life. We may be insecure about our existence and rely too much on material prosperity. When we become too involved with "me, myself and I," we become entombed in our own world. The tragedy here is that the beauty of life and the fresh winds of vitality come to us as we give of ourselves in love and care for others; not as we live merely for ourselves. How often have we heard it is more blessed to give than to receive." Believe it or not, IT IS!

Jesus said to a very rich man one time, "You can gain the whole world and lose your soul." The need to please ourselves often drives us to use people for our own gain and pleasure. A Jewish philosopher, Martin Buber wrote, "We humans often love things and use people. We are challenged to love people and use things." In order for this to happen we truly have to die to self before we can share in the resurrected life. Jesus also reminds us that a seed must fall into the ground and die before the plant can grow and flourish. So it is with our own lives; we must let those deadly passions for self die, so that the new life God breathes into us will grow and flourish.

Easter is a great celebration of this possibility of new life that the risen Christ offers to all who believe. It is a recognition that we don't have to be afraid of not being someday. The Apostle Paul wrote: "O death where is thy sting, O grave where is thy victory. Thanks be to God who gives us the victory in Christ." Because He lives, we can not only face, but claim, tomorrow.

Turn the Page

MARCH 25, 2008

Last week, I was on the way to have lunch with my son. As I drove along, my thoughts closed in on what as I going to do with the rest of my life. I have been retired 10 years. What a decade that has been. I have watched my grandchildren blossom into young people.

Becky, my wife, and I have enjoyed excellent health. I have had many opportunities to continue serving my Lord in the church. And this fabulously diverse world has unfolded before Becky and me as we have traveled to so many places on his globe.

These guiding "thoughts" I would use for my life are useful for all of us at whatever juncture we may find ourselves. Think about the many transitions in life! Many generational changes occur. Children take that initial journey to school. Young adults leave home and enter the adult world. There is the transition from work to retirement. In life and in death we are faced with tragedies and accomplishments which call for major adjustments. With every critical moment in time, we are given that wonderful opportunity to chart a new and fresh direction for the "living of these days."

Unfortunately, we often choose to continue "business as usual". The common and ordinary become comfortable. Rather than settling for this, we need to reach for the uncommon and the extraordinary. I have always been impressed with the Apostle Paul's words when he cast off his past with all of its accomplishments. He said, "I am not perfect, I have not arrived, but press on to this new life [my high calling] I have found in Christ." This new life is captured for me on the stage of life in such words as love and justice. Let me suggest that we become comfortable in the common and ordinary and strike a death note when we are so "involved in ourselves". We are able to press on and strike a life note when and where we become strategically involved in the well being of others and the enhancement of society.

Getting Ready

APRIL 16, 2008

Following the rains comes the day of sun and warm temperatures. Today was a lovely day to get in the yard and continue preparation for Spring planting and Summer growing. Our back yard has multiple flower beds where my wife enjoys planting for new life and beauty. But in order for such planting to happen, the flower beds need preparation. We have found that the beauty of the blooming flowers requires (using a human term) the tender care for the soil.

This time of preparation reminds me of the many happenings along the human journey that require preparation. For example, the life of a child reaching adulthood is cultivated along the way with the constant nurture of parents and the help of the extended community. With such care and support, the next door through which the child passes becomes an open passage to the future and not a brick wall that keeps the child in the past.

Each stage in this human journey realizes optimal fulfillment when we have diligently prepared for that stage. One of my favorite quotes is by Robert Browning from "Rabbi Ben Ezra". These are the words: "Grow old along with me, the best is yet to be; the last for which the first was meant." Also, each stage in life gives shape and meaning, so we can effectively live the next stage.

Don't get me wrong! I am not suggesting that life is one continuous exercise in preparation. Not at all! When we live each stage of our lives with meaning and fullness, then we will be truly ready for the next stage. Being aware of what we need for the next stage in life is essential.

Maybe we've not fully prepared ourselves along the way. I don't believe it is ever too late to call "time out" if we are just living for the moment with no thought of a tomorrow, with no real preparation going on. The Apostle Paul made reference to a lifestyle solely concerned with the moment with the words: "Let's eat, drink and be merry for tomorrow we may die." Sure, we are going to die some day, but even death calls for preparation, if not for ourselves, for those we love.

Wherever you are along your human journey and if you are just bidding time, living merely for the usual and ordinary, take a "time out" and begin preparing today so tomorrow will be a new and significant day for you, not just another day along life's weary way. It's never too late.

Maintenance

MAY 27, 2008

My thoughts reach to a day 50 years back. I was visiting with Senator Fulbright [Arkansas] in his office, in Washington D.C. Our nation was in the midst of the war in Vietnam. A serious garbage strike was underway in New York City. The garbage was piling up on the streets of the city. You would have thought that the war would have been the center of our conversation, but it was not. Senator Fulbright at that time was more concerned with the garbage strike. He said, "We tend to forget how important garbage collectors are to the health and welfare of a city." The people who keep our communities regularly operating and routinely clean are valuable. Unfortunately, we tend to take a well-organized and working community for granted, and in turn, the maintenance people. Maybe, I should say to all of these people, before I forget, "Thanks for making our community a better place to live."

It's taken me almost 75 years to reach a conscious recognition of the value of the role of maintenance. Since my retirement, I spend much more time in the yard weeding the flower beds, cutting the grass, and trimming the hedges. At one time in my life, I would have performed these actions with much resistance. But today, these activities let me share with my wife in creating a beautiful natural environment around us.

I remember those days when I engaged in regular counseling. Some people would complain about these routine activities. My advice to them would be to think about the contribution the activity under question would make in helping those around them or improving their surroundings. Such a mental exercise is beneficial. But even more notable is when we reach the point in life when these so-called maintenance activities are done with joy.

Yes, I have reached the age when I have to take a few more pills and engage in a regular exercise program. All of this is done not merely to stay alive, but to keep the body in shape. Our ability to enjoy life is directly related to our physical health, and also to our mental and spiritual, health. It becomes a bit of an effort to take the pills and exercise regularly, yet, when I realize that the outcome is a more vital life, it is all worthwhile. I have come to the conclusion that God wants me to keep myself healthy, not just for my enjoyment, but so I can live a life of love and justice as I reach out with concern for others.

When God created the world, the scriptures read that after six days God took time to reflect and that with reflection, God declared, "It is good." We have been placed in the midst of creation and have been commanded to take care of the creation, enjoy it and share in the creativity of the world. Let's remember that creativity and maintenance are two sides of the same coin; you can't have one without the other.

Memories

JUNE 17, 2008

"Memories, memories ..." are the words from a song that comes to mind. When I retired 10 years ago, I found myself reflecting on the journey that I had taken over the years. I think of the words of Ecclesiastes in the Bible, "There is a time to be born and a time to die." This passage of scripture goes on to describe many differing experiences of time. My reflections carried me back through the years along many paths and up, what I call, many rabbit trails. I learned much about myself as I have reclaimed memories of my life's journey.

Let me suggest that there is great value in recapturing our memories. We come to understand that what happens to us is not a random assortment of events. Rather, there is a pattern that is displayed -- a thread that seems to tie these events together, yes, the unfolding purpose for our life.

I often quote something my mother spoke to me when I was extremely young. She said, "Sam, God has created you with a plan and purpose for your life." Capturing the memories of my past has enabled me to see more clearly God's purpose for my life. In the broadest sense of the word, my purpose has been to "Glorify God and enjoy Him forever." In the more specific sense of the word, my purpose has been to be a facilitator for the rights of all people, in the ways of my Lord, Jesus Christ. This does not preclude my role as husband and parent and pastor where I believe God has given me the grace of being a caring person.

Enough about me! I have walked you through my own journey to encourage you to remember events and relationships in your life, but not merely to remember, but to capture your memories to discover the pattern of your life or the thread that brings all that together. Why? There is an additional serendipity that happens which is an insight into your unfolding future. What you have done and where you have been can be immensely helpful in guiding you into what you are becoming. Let me once again refer to one of my favorite quotes [from Rabbi Ben Ezra by Browning] *"Grow old along with me, the best is yet to be; the last for which the first was meant."*

Something practical has to be said at this point. These two exercises are helpful in recalling the events in your life: keep an ongoing journal and keep a picture album. These so-called tools will help you reflect with reasonable clarity. But these tools will also be ways in which your children and grandchildren can get to know you. I have accumulated seven picture albums that tell my life's story; also my family's story. Every time my grandchildren visit Becky and me, they will pull out some of the albums and browse through them with much delight.

This life which God has given each of us is so beautiful and precious, despite some of the pain we might endure or difficulties we face along the way. Please don't move through life so fast that you lose touch with it. Pause along the way to capture the precious moments, so you can recall the abiding beauty of your life. "Take time to smell the roses." It is never too late to begin!

Life, Liberty, Happiness

JULY 2, 2008

In several days, we will be celebrating Independence Day. Just over 230 years ago, the resounding cry of freedom was heard throughout the land. The note was struck – "All men are created equal and endowed by their Creator with certain inalienable rights of life, liberty and the pursuit of happiness."

The Bible is a terrific story of a creator God who wishes well for his creation. Even when we humans seem to do our best to mess things up, God does not forsake us. Even when we want to build fences around our own compounds to keeps others out and hold on to what we have, God does not forsake us. There is a repeated theme throughout the Holy Book to "be not dismayed what'er betide, God will take care of you."

This is not to say that we do not reap destruction in the whirlwind because of our dastardly ways toward each other and our abuse of the creation. The thought that I would like to share is we tend to engage each other out of our own self interests rather than our mutual interests. The outcome often lacks a profound and far-reaching collage where all of the people share in the blessings of life, liberty and the pursuit of happiness.

So may I bring you back to the words … "created equal and endowed by their creator. We are truly a nation of many religions, but I would suggest just one God. The one living and true God has created all of us. The living and true God holds us together despite our efforts to live in our separate enclaves. We pledge "one nation under God with liberty and justice for all". What our human minds, we fashion our images of God in different thoughts and forms; the one true God is the creator and sustainer of the whole of humanity. Herein lies the hope for a world free of division and strife, where we "lay down our swords and shields, and study war no more."

It is my belief that Jesus came, in the words of the Apostle Paul, to tear down the walls created by human minds and passions. Jesus calls upon us, not to turn our backs on those with whom we differ, but to accept them as people of value and worth, created by the one true God. This is the God Jesus invites us to worship. Jesus offers us freedom from the divisions and strife of this world, not only salvation into eternity.

Let me offer an appeal! This Independence Day celebration calls us to a freedom from any religion that limits our ability to worship the sovereign God of all humanity and embrace each other in mutual care. Out of such a frame of reference we can live with a greater assurance that life, liberty and the pursuit of happiness for all people will become a growing reality.

Change

JULY 30, 2008

We hear a lot about change lately! The two persons who are running for president are trying to capitalize on the dissatisfaction of the American electorate. They are suggesting a change from where we are to where they think we should be. I am beginning my thoughts with this point of reference because the notion of change is in the wind and on our lips. So I invite you to explore the notion of change with me.

Change is not only in the wind and on our lips, but change is real. In the human journey, we have gone far beyond the belief in a static universe or the status quo. Each season of the year gives way to the next not only with change, but also with order. With every new invention and insight, change touches our lives. We change from active children to deliberate aging adults. Our families change from a nest of busy children to an empty nest. Happenings all around us cause life to change for the good and for the bad. Time and life are like an ever rolling stream. Change is within us.

The issue before us is not simply change. If I were to invite a sharing of opinions, these would be many in number and thought. There are essential notes to strike by asking two questions. "First, what is changing and how do we go about dealing with such change?" The second note concerns "what is it that we need to change and why?" We can't stop change! We might want to freeze our lives in time, particularly at that time of rapturous moments and notable accomplishments. Let me suggest that those moments and accomplishments should be captured in memory and become springboards for the emerging tomorrow. We don't want to become frozen in time, because we would miss so much of the unfolding future.

I would like to leave you with some practical thoughts [not all encompassing, by any means] about dealing with change, particularly as you live out of the past and move into the future. We hold on to the past to our detriment. We learn from the past to our gain. I recall a history professor saying, "Remembering the past helps us not make the same mistakes in the future." And that's so true, isn't it? I use an exercise with my grandchildren by asking them after they have had a certain experience, "What have your learned? What have you learned about others? About yourself? About the world, in which you live?" Take what you have learned, use these learnings as you make your steps into the future! I am reminded of the words of Jesus, "You can gain the whole world and lose your soul; you can die to yourself [accept and give shape to change] and find life."

I think it might be appropriate to cite a few words from the song by M. Jagger/K. Richards, Time Waits for No One. *"Drink in your summer, gather your corn. The dreams of the night time will vanish by dawn. And time waits for no one, and it won't wait for me. And time waits for no one, and it won't wait for thee."*

"So pack up your trouble in your old kit bag, and smile, smile, smile." [World War I, Marching Song]

The Olympics Speak

SEPTEMBER 3, 2008

Over the last several weeks, I have been glued to the TV watching the Olympics. It is impressive how these young adults from all over the world has displayed the character and determination of a winner. How often was it said that even if a person did not win a medal, just getting to the Olympics was an accomplishment. Everybody cannot be number one, but everybody can be a winner, particularly in an arena where there is such respect for each other. The Olympics is such an arena! Of course, from time to time you would see a offensive outburst, but that was the exception, not the rule.

An approach to interpersonal relationships comes to mind. It is called "I'm OK, You're OK." This way of dealing with life has the goal to produce situations where we are all winners. One person or a group may be first or establish a more strategic position, but being a winner is never done with the desire to destroy the other. Also, being a winner includes a keen appreciation for the talents, efforts and assets of those with whom we compete. A significant part of group competition is congratulating the persons on the opposite team at the end of the play. Jesus was a person who called for the open door of caring love even for the enemy. Also, Apostle Paul, building on

29

Jesus' words, often stressed the importance of "giving greater consideration to the other person than you do for yourself." This essential approach to life is rooted in the belief that God is sovereign over all of life. We find in a familiar song these words: "He's got the whole world in his hands. He's got you and me in his hands ..."

The resounding point I am trying to set forth is when we have respect for others, particularly those with whom we disagree or in competition with, we will go a long way toward living together in peace. Even though we may be the winner, we don't look upon the other person as a loser. And when this is the way everybody "plays the game of life," the level of satisfied living on this planet earth will be elevated.

As we approach the election of a president and other people for public office, I would hope that the behavior at the Olympics would provide guidance to all of us. In the final analysis, we perhaps want to go a step further and remember that we need each other to achieve the goal of "life, liberty and the pursuit of happiness" for all. In some ways, our personal lives are diminished when we don't play the game of life in this manner.

I was impressed with the mile relay team. Each of the men ran separately in the quarter mile race; they competed to be the winner. Together, they ran the mile relay and competed together to be a team of winners. Life is more like running as a relay team. They could not win unless each did his/her part in the race. We can't win the race of life unless we all do our part with realized respect for and dependence upon each other. When this happens, we are all winners. Life truly becomes a many splendored thing.

Someone to know ... Something to do ... A place to go!

SEPTEMBER 10, 2008

I have made reference to words of my mother in a previous article. When I was young, my mother would often say to me, "Don't forget Sam, God has a plan and purpose for your life." This belief has carried me through each year and the ongoing journey of my life. Now, as I reach the winter years of life, I ask the question, "How do these words from my mother speak to me today?" I imagine that most of you who have reached what we call the senior years might be asking this same question. I would like to help you [and me] in this musing over the meaning of life in these twilight years. Although, what I am about to write has much to say to anyone at any stage of life.

My initial thoughts are focused on a relative in the twilight years of his life. He has been ill for the last five years or more. He is a little older than I am, but he has progressively reached the point in his life where he mostly sits and watches TV. When his children were young, he would get on the floor and play with them. He cared for his family. He was a devoted husband and father. He was never a gregarious person but had an interest in the people around him. His interest in history carried him outside of himself and the people around him. As he began to lose his independence, indicated in the loss of his driver's license, you could see his claim on life gradually fading. Just recently, he has had a stroke and lies a bit docile in a hospital bed. We prayerfully hope that fresh energy will flow into his body, and he will have some good days ahead of him.

This "life happening" that I have shared with you brings to mind the question, "How does he live out God's plan and purpose for his life?" Of course, this question needs to be asked long before we face the deterioration of aging, namely as we approach retirement. Long before we reach this stage, we need three conditions of life to claim the blessings of life: someone to know ... something to do ... a place to go. Actually, these conditions are critical throughout our entire life ~ from birth to death.

It's fun to let the mind take a thought or a question and explore the results. As I played with this question "How does he live out God's ...?" My mind produced these three phrases ~ Someone to know ...Something to do ... A place to go. Each of these phrases gives us the springboard for another article. So let me encourage you to think on these phrases regarding you own life.

My relative, mentioned above had someone to know, but not beyond his immediate family ... he had nothing to do ... and he was very limited in where he could go. The outcome was a diminishing world resulting in a diminishing self. Maybe those of us who live with family members or friends like this can help provide meaning to their lives by providing them with someone to know ... something to do ... and a place to go. What a gift we would be giving them for the diminishing time they have!

Do you have someone to know ... something to do ... a place to go?

Something to Do

SEPTEMBER 24, 2008

The recent foundational article grew out of the observation of an aging family member whose world had collapsed into a small space of existence. I began to reflect on what it is that we humans need in order to sustain a life of meaning. The outcome of my reflections grew into the above title. I want to reflect now on what it means to have "something to do." Last time, we thought through what it means to have "someone to know."

As I mentioned in the initial article, my family member's world narrowed to his home where he spent most of his time watching TV, which is not all together bad. His lifestyle before he became limited in his activities included going to his office; before he retired he was in real-estate and sold farm land. His work gave him something constructive to do and provided interaction with others. He was not a person who worked around the home much. After he retired, he would go to his office and visit his friends. The lack of something to do at home took its toll on his vitality and personal engagement. The outcome was a diminishing world resulting in a diminishing self.

How vital it is to have something to do! I'm sure you know people who have been confined to their home and yet find something to do that keeps them involved in life and engaged with the world. We all have interests, hobbies and abilities that when used can be life-giving. How vital it is not only to exercise the body, but also the mind and the spirit! I think the key to "the something we do" is how much does whatever we do enable us to interact with the world. This interaction is with the world outside of ourselves where we become a conduit of God's love to others; yes, and to be engaged with God in whom we live and move and have our being.

Jesus summed up the commandments Moses received on the mountain with the words, "Love God with your whole being and your neighbor as yourself." So we might suggest that simply doing something to occupy our time may be enriching, but allowing the "Spirit of love" to use our hearts to care and our arms to serve becomes life-giving.

As our world narrows, the opportunities to serve others become fewer and fewer. Because of this narrowing, it is essential for those of us who are able to become care-givers and life-givers to those whose worlds are diminishing. We should not only help keep them busy, but also help keep them interactive. Jesus said, "If you've done it to one of the least of these my brothers, you have done it unto me." The least are not only the children, but also those who find their world becoming smaller. They need to have someone to be their support system where they are able to claim life as long as they have breath.

My final thought might be, "what we do for others is just as essential as what we do for ourselves if we are going to claim life fully."

Some Place to Go

SEPTEMBER 30, 2008

This builds on the article that grew out of the observation of an aging family member whose world had collapsed into a small space of existence. This time, I want to complete these articles with "Some Place to Go."

Before the subject of the story retired, he sold farm land for a profession. He had a place to go. His work gave him something productive to do and provided interaction with others. When he stopped driving and became dependent on others to provide a place to go, his world began to diminish.

Why is having a place to go important? First, let me deal with this question from a negative point of view. When we are confined to one place, we are inclined to experience a narrowing of perspective. We tend to lose interest, not only in the world beyond us, but also in the people around us. Our world becomes smaller and smaller, confined to "me, myself and I." With such a narrowing of perspective, preoccupation with our personal needs claims us more and more.

Second, having spoken negatively, let's examine the importance of reaching out beyond ourselves where we have a place to go. It's hard to think about a place to go without including "someone to know" and "something to do." When anyone steps out the backdoor of one's house and engages the world, even if it is just that familiar day to day place, a certain freedom to reach out touches one's life. This freedom allows us to see the sun beyond the clouds and gain fresh life in the interaction with the people around us. This freedom to engage life grows and grows when we venture into new places near and far.

Even when we are confined to a limited place because of our physical health, we still can fly with the eagles and run with the horses where we are able to see and to claim this marvelous world. Children, whose worlds are usually limited, become exposed to a larger world as they are encouraged to read; we can continue to have a place to go between the covers of a good book. Over the last 10 years, my wife and I have had the privilege of traveling to many places in the world; these many places have given breath and depth to our lives. The day will come when we will no longer be able to do this. Yet there will always be books, magazines and newspapers that give us places to go … the pictures and videos give an extended reach of places to see.

I would be amiss without affirming that "This is our Father's world and to our listening ears, all nature sings and round us rings the music of the spheres." Beyond what we can experience with our senses there is the infinite expanse of the spiritual universe; our world will never diminish as we "walk with the Lord in the light of his way."

What About that Old Man!

OCTOBER 22, 2008

It is fascinating how much the news media makes reference to Senator McCain's age. He will be the oldest person who has run for the presidency. I think to myself, "Well, we are adding another prejudice, namely, age prejudice."

What have we come to in our society? In some of the societies that we condemn for their lack of democracy, we find a serious level of respect for the aging. Yet in our so-called democratic society ~ this land of the brave and home of the free ~ we find our comedians and political commentators seemingly showing little respect for the aged or aging.

Of course, I realize that it is not best to generalize. I am 75 years old and have experienced much respect. All of my grandchildren [five in number] say "Yes sir" and "No sir" in response to me. As I move about in the community and interact with people, the word, "sir" comes dropping from the lips of those younger than I. I have made it a habit these days to engage people in conversation. The word amazing might be appropriate in describing the many delightful responses I have received. Let me share with you a conversation I just had yesterday while getting into my car after going to the movie.

There was a younger man, much younger, probably more like middle age. He had just gotten onto his motorcycle, a beautiful piece of equipment, and was putting on his helmet. I said to him, "That sure is a neat motorcycle." His face lit up with the response, "Thank you." I then proceeded to tell him about my aborted intentions to buy two motorcycles. When my son graduated from high school, I thought about taking a month off to ride with him throughout the country. This would have been an exciting venture for me and my son. It would have fulfilled his desire to have a cycle and my attempt to enjoy his company for a time before he went to college. The man responded, "I am planning to do this with my 25 year old son in the near future. Hope this will help us bond." Well I never bought the cycles. At the time, it would have been a nice thing to do, although we have become well-bonded over the years since then.

I have often thought of myself as a young man in an old body. I would like to suggest that young and old in the usual sense of the words have nothing to do -- yet everything to do with the vitality of life. A key notion, regardless of age, is to enjoy life by engaging people along our earthly journey. Don't forget from that the day we are born we are moving into the sunset of life. One of the greatest joys is found in the people we meet along the way.

A New Beginning

DECEMBER 3, 2008

Everybody likes the opportunity of a new beginning! We have just begun the Advent Season in the life of the Christian faith. Too often, we celebrate Christmas with no thought of Advent. Have you ever said, "The merchants are rolling out Christmas before we have even observed Thanksgiving." Well, I am going to say, "We have forgotten Advent as we rush into Christmas."

Why is it necessary to celebrate Advent before we plunge into Christmas? In so many ways, Christmas is the celebration of the gift of new life in the birth of the Christ child. As the prophet Isaiah wrote presciently some 750 years before the Nativity, "The people who walked in darkness have seen a great light." While Christmas represents the beginning of a new age in God's management of life, it is the culmination of "the hopes and dreams of all the years being met in Jesus that night."

The people of Israel had been promised a Messiah, the one who would deliver them from their repeated oppression. In the greater scheme of life, this promise was deliverance from sin and death that imprisons all of humanity in the claws of destructive proclivities. With this promise embedded in their psyche, they survived the daily ups and downs of life with the anticipation of the Messiah. Anticipation enhances and enriches the happening when it occurs. Christmas becomes an impactful event in our lives when it comes after a season of rich anticipation … the anticipation that all will be well with life.

Anticipation is the measure out of which hope takes shape. How much we need to keep hope alive! Yes, particularly in today's world. The tsunamis of terrorism and nature, and now economics have wreaked havoc on all of us sojourners, some more than others, on the spaceship Earth. We need a time, such as Christmas and the weeks leading up to Christmas that will tell the story of deliverance. This story has been written in the "sands of time and echoed from the voices of the prophets and embraced in the human hearts as an everlasting melody of hope.

This is what it means to live in hope. Keep hope alive! Keep hope alive with the image of this most notable event to happen in our lives. This event has formed in our hearts ~ is envisioned in our minds ~ becomes the possibility realization in our future. Let me share with you words from the Wizard of Oz, which capture this note of hope:

> "Somewhere, over the rainbow, way up high
> There's a land that I heard of once in lullaby.
> Somewhere, over the rainbow, skies are blue,
> And the dreams that you dare to dream really
> do come true."

Breaking Out in the New Year

JANUARY 7, 2009

Several weeks ago, I saw the movie, *The Curious Case of Benjamin Button*. This is the saga of a person who ages backward, from senility to virile adulthood, and then to childhood. The opening scenes involved a clockmaker who was building a clock for the train terminal. When put in place and started, the clock operated backward. The clockmaker commented to everyone that he intentionally built the clock to move backward. He was in the hope that his son, killed in World War I would be reclaimed from history and given the opportunity to live a long and prosperous life.

The opportunity to live a long and prosperous life is something we all want. But longevity without a sense of fulfillment produces an empty life. Also, prosperity without sharing produces a lonely life.

The beginning of a new year is the time that we at least look back to reflect on where we have been. This backward look hopefully becomes a springboard where we are able to launch our new year. Regrets are set aside. Unfulfilled dreams may be revisited. More than likely, our goal is to live a long and prosperous life, if not a healthy and balanced life.

Some may want to go back in time where the basis of our regrets might be reshaped so that today would be different. We can't go back. The only direction we can go is forward. As I have often said, "Today can be the first day of a new life." "What am I going to do with this new life?" becomes the critical question.

Are you going to live life solely in terms of the cycle of life, adding another year to the calendar as you march toward the end of your earthly existence? Or are you going to break out of the cycle and engage in a new and fresh dimension of living? Breaking out or hanging on is the question. Do most of us just hang on? Every trip I take … every new book I read … every new challenge I respond to … every new project I undertake … every person I am able to help … every one of these gives me the opportunity to break out of the orbit of the existence I am in … and wow, what a day it will be.

How often have you heard people [or maybe even yourself] say, "It sure would be nice to be young again!" My wife's response to this notion is "Not me … I like who I am … where I am." There is something exciting about living an unfolding life, rather than a regressing life. As I have often quoted [Browning in Rabbi Ben Ezra] *"Grow old along with me. The best is yet to be, the last for which the first was meant."* Life is a progression toward something, not away from something. Life provides unfolding opportunities to be a person of value; to be in touch with the love, the justice and the glory of God.

In Life and Death We Belong to God

JANUARY 21, 2009

We are beginning a new year. We learn from the writer of Ecclesiastes that "there is a time to be born and a time to die." During the last several weeks, the Oakland Presbyterian congregation has experienced both death and new life.

A member of our congregation died after a period of illness and decreasing health. He was a faithful member of this congregation and the church universal. We have celebrated his life with us and rejoiced for his life with God in eternity. We have embraced his wife and extended family with our love and support.

During this same time, a child was born to a couple that has been attending worship. They blessed us with the presence of their daughter the Sunday after her birth. We celebrated the birth of our Lord three days after this child was born. We want to thank God for the presence of this young family in our midst and give glory to God for this new life. It is renewing to hear a baby's cry in the silence of worship.

In this period of time, death and life have been experienced and cherished. We must always affirm that in "life and death" we belong to God. Each and every Sunday together we are privileged to celebrate this life when we worship. Apart from God who has created us and given us new life in Christ, we would not be. We have heard the words over and over: "In God, we live and move and have our being."

Francis Havergal wrote these lyrics for a hymn: "Lord speak to me that I may speak in living echoes of Thy voice ..." In life and death we not only belong to God, but in life and death [and all the other times in our life] God speaks to us. We come to know and then to recognize God speaking to us of the meaning of life, found in His holy embrace and lived out in our earthly journey. The words of a song come to mind as we recognize the voice of eternity along our time framed journey: "Every time I hear a new born baby cry or touch a leaf or see the sky I know why I believe." The word of God has become flesh in Jesus Christ. The word of God also becomes flesh in so many other significant ways. Be sensitive to God's voice as you hear him pass in the rustling grass; he speaks to you everywhere.

A Venture Outside of the Common and Ordinary

FEBRUARY 25, 2009

Several weeks ago, I wrote an article entitled, "Putting on Holy Glasses." I invited us to explore different ways to look at life. The first way was described as "black and white." The second way was in Technicolor. And finally, I suggested that, beyond the absolutes and variations, there is the spiritual dimension of life where we look at life through "Holy Glasses." Of course, when we look through "Holy Glasses," the evidence of God's providential presence and activity comes into sharp focus.

Since I wrote that article, my thoughts have been pondering over several other images. These might be helpful in breaking out of the way we normally do things. We go through life from day to day living within the confines of the common and ordinary. When we do this, we seldom go beneath and beyond where we've always been. We become lost in either no light or too much light. When this happens, we miss the variations and shades that bring vibrancy.

Let's talk about this vast world in which we live. At one time, the earth was described as having four corners. Then we learned that it was round and rotated around the sun in a galaxy in a universe of many galaxies. With the telescope, we have been introduced to the macro world, the vast universe of which we are a part. With the microscope, we are introduced to the micro world, the extremely small structures of creation. Both of these worlds truly exist, but we are unable to see or explore them with the normal human tools of exploration.

There is so much to learn that we are unable to know along the common and ordinary ways of life. This is not only true of the created order, but it is also true of what we might call the spiritual order of life. I was taught as a young child that "God is a spirit and has not a body like man." We humans are not only part of this earthly creation, but we are also part of the spiritual world where the true reality of our existence is revealed and realized. The Bible describes us as temples of the Holy Spirit. Our body is but the earthen vessel that enables us to live and move and have our being as part of this earthly existence. This is why we put on our Holy Glasses. With these glasses, we not only see and experience the creation with all of its splendor and beauty, but experience the creator in all of God's majesty and wonder.

Remember that you are Dust

MARCH 11, 2009

Several weeks ago, we celebrated Ash Wednesday at the Oakland Presbyterian Church. In a highly visible way, Ash Wednesday marks the beginning of Lent, when we take stock and prepare ourselves for the journey toward Easter. Believers across the globe go to church where they can participate in what is called the Imposition of Ashes. The priest or the minister dips his finger into a bowl of burnt ashes, makes the sign of the cross on your forehead and says, "Remember that you are dust, and to dust you shall return."

Someone has written about Ash Wednesday. "For years, I was tremendously comforted by the thought that God knew me, loved me, and accepted me, but I did not give equal attention to the other side of the equation: that being, the need to face my darker nature, name it, and seek forgiveness. I didn't realize how naïve, even arrogant, I was being."

When we are able to face our darker nature, the beauty of God's creation in us begins to blossom. Such an encounter with our darker side is possible because of God's love and acceptance. The words of the Psalmist come to mind: *"Have mercy on me, O God, according to your loving-kindness; in your great compassion blot out my offenses."* *(Psalm 51:1) King David wrote this psalm after he had committed a particularly grievous sin. After this initial appeal to God, and the realization of God's forgiveness; he implored God to give him a new heart and he would give praise to God before all the people.*

In the broad realm of healthy living, we are brought in touch with the truth that failure to recognize and give up our dark side can be destructive to our relationships with others, not to mention our own emotional health. It is overwhelming how much of our destructive behavior toward others and ourselves comes from unresolved issues in our personal lives. We don't like who we are and so we bury this dislike deep, deep within our inner self. And these unresolved issues become compounded ... they fester in us. They become like a hammer or sword in our hands as we relate to others.

We've often heard "confession is good for the soul." Well it is! These buried lumps of darkness need to be removed before we can breathe the fresh air of a new day. Removed, before we can treat others with respect and care. Removed, before we find the blessings of the joy of living. A Season of Lent is essential. It's like cleaning house. We give ourselves definite time to get rid of what we have accumulated in our inner self that is of little value ... actually, that is hampering our lives. So take time in this Lenten Season to take a look at your life in the light of God's loving-kindness. And as it has often been said, "You will not regret it!"

Life as a Journey

APRIL 8, 2009

My dear friends, I often speak of life as a journey. Several Sundays ago, I made reference to this thought and suggested different ways of viewing our journey. We all are on a journey from birth to death. Framed within this earthly journey is our engagement with God, which gives an eternal dimension to this earthly venture.

The good note about this journey is that God has defined certain times such as Sunday to help us allow time to reflect on the meaning of this journey. The bad note is that we often choose to disregard the opportunity for worship and Godly reflection. The real tragedy is that we get captured by a routine of life that freezes us in time. Frozen in time, we become paralyzed and unable to breathe the fresh air of God's eternal presence.

We also have what is called the "Church Year" which begins with the birth of Christ [Christmas] and moves through Palm Sunday, Holy Week and Easter. We are in that most exciting time of the year, Palm Sunday, Holy Week and Easter. We, so to speak, become participants with Jesus in His journey to the Cross and His Resurrection. This is a glorious time for us, became we are able to say "the strife is o'er, the battle done; the victory of life is won."

But when we fail to take advantage of our times of worship we remain, as I mentioned, frozen in time. We then miss a real opportunity to be claimed by the fresh winds of a new day, and lifted up into the sunshine of God is resurrected presence.

Our Lord took his journey to the cross in order that we might be saved from sin and death; it is sad when we remain frozen in time, never giving ourselves the opportunity to travel with our Lord into the sunshine of eternity. How unfortunate it is when we remain stuck in the rut of repetitive living. So let's be sure we come together with our Lord on Easter Sunday to be reminded that "THE LORD IS RAISED … HE IS RAISED INDEED. Let us do this with deep care that we all share not merely in the passing seasons but in the glimpse of eternity.

Survival!!!

APRIL 29, 2009

I have in my mind a picture and in that picture is a capsized boat. Two men are hanging onto the sides of the boat. The water is splashing against the boat and over the men. They find themselves to be tossed back and forth in the choppy sea. We would use the word ~ survival ~ to describe the outcome of this circumstance.

A person does not have to be hanging onto a capsized boat in a choppy sea to be caught in the grips of survival. We can be living in the lap of luxury or in a village with only one water pump and find ourselves merely surviving from day to day. I conducted a funeral recently. The next day, I began to reflect on the paths a person might take after the death of a loved one. The bereaved, gripped with remorse, might lapse into a survival routine. They could find themselves to be living from day to day, only doing what is necessary to stay alive.

I would call this "a survival mode." We do whatever we need to do, and no more, just to stay alive. When we do this, we have given in to what has happened and have rejected the possibility of a new day. On the other hand, we might acknowledge we are [as we read in the 23rd Psalm] "walking through the valley of the shadow of death … we will fear no evil [or destruction] for God is with us" and we will come onto the verdant pastures of the new day.

Would you say that it is easier to survive than to "get up and get with it?" Survival is finding a comfort zone in our life and staying there. I have observed that we humans have a tendency sometimes to accept downright damnable situations because we lack "whatever it is" to stand upright and move out. We cause ourselves to believe that a hellish situation is better than nothing because we don't know where to go or what to do. Such a posture in life is mere survival, nothing more, nothing less.

In order to get a handle on this notion of survival, we might explore a variety of situations such as the person whose loved one has died. He continues to live in the initial stage of shock and does what is necessary just to stay alive from day to day … the lady who is knocked around by an abusive husband remains in the situation … the individual who has difficulty getting around and spends all of his time in front of the TV. For these and many others who merely survive, the value of each hour is lost and the days roll over into the oblivion of tomorrow. And then someday we die.

Survival or revival becomes the question of the day! And in the words of Paul Harvey, next week you will read the rest of the story!

In Remembrance

MAY 27, 2009

Memorial Day is a United States federal holiday observed on the last Monday of May. It commemorates U.S. men and women who died while in the military service; first enacted, to honor Union soldiers of the American Civil War. After World War I, it was expanded to include American casualties of any war or military action. Many people observe this holiday by visiting cemeteries and memorials. A national moment of remembrance takes place at 3 p.m. Eastern Time. Another tradition is to fly the flag of the United States at half-staff from dawn until noon local time. Volunteers often put American flags on each gravesite at National cemeteries. Many Americans also use Memorial Day to honor other family members who have died.

Why is it so necessary to remember those who have died to defend our country? I am reminded of a story about a soldier who woke up in a hospital after being wounded. The first words from his mouth were, "Where is Johnny?" Johnny was his best friend and an Army buddy. The doctor responded "Johnny was killed. He crawled out into the field where you had been wounded and brought you back. While bringing you back, he was wounded. The soldier wept as he responded, "He gave his life, so I could live." The men and women of the military have given their lives, so we can live.

Memorial Day is about commitment and sacrifice. People who are willing to sacrifice their lives for a grand and noble cause show a genuine commitment. They believe that their cause is more valuable than their life. We realize a strong, productive and creative society when people are willing to be more a giver than a consumer. The real challenge today is for the heart of a true soldier to become the heart of more Americans. Instead of simply building "more stately mansions for me, myself and I," let's be equally concerned for the well being of "all the people, all the time."

An appropriate Memorial Day celebration looks forward as well as backward. We remember with respect and appreciation those who have died for righteousness and freedom. We look forward with personal commitment to "life, liberty and the pursuit of happiness." In this world, there is much goodness and light. The challenge is to turn from the bad and the dark to the good and the light. This challenge is not only for ourselves, but for all people to give our best to ensure the dawning of this new day.

Where it all Began

OCTOBER 7, 2009

My wife and I are home once again, after traveling over 14,000 miles. These last two weeks, we have visited "Where It All Began." Our first stop on the marathon journey was Israel, then on to Jordan and Egypt before returning home by way of Rome, Italy. When I visit other places, particularly outside of the United States, I try to go with an open mind and not see the people and places I visit through the lenses of my life here in the United States.

The first part of the trip gave us the opportunity to "walk with the Lord" as he ministered to the people in Galilee, then on to Bethlehem where Jesus was born. We spent three days in Jerusalem and journeyed with Jesus to the upper room where he had his last Passover meal with his disciples, then on to the Garden of Gethsemane. From there, we followed the steps of Jesus through his trial and his crucifixion. Just imagine sailing on the Sea of Galilee where Jesus calmed the waters; we were there -- this place where the faithful and not so faithful can touch reality and find a special blessing.

Our guide, an archeologist for this part of the trip, told us that her parents had come to Israel from Iraq before she was born. Her rich knowledge of the excavation of Jerusalem to reclaim the past and her passion for the truth helped us understand more clearly the history and the way of the Jewish people ... their customs and religion ... their passion for life and determination to exist.

We visited the site of the first temple built by Solomon. Now stands on that site a Muslim place of worship, not to mention these buildings have been built on the rock of Mount Moriah where God commanded Abraham to take his son Isaac to be offered as a sacrifice. I came to realize why Jerusalem was so vital to the Jews. This was the place where God gathered them in times past and continues to remind them of his eternal presence. For the Muslims, this is the place where they too are reminded of their connection to the rock from which they were hewn. This also is the place where Muslim, Jew and Christian find their common identity with the Lord God of all.

I don't have time to take you on our full journey, but I would like to share with you our time in Egypt with our guide as he brought us in touch with the greatness of a past that has been unearthed. The temples and pyramids built thousands and thousands of years past, and recently unearthed helped me become aware of the past splendor and destructive ways of humankind, a splendor and destructiveness that continues to this day. I have come to appreciate even more my human journey and divine engagement.

A journey into the past with an open and searching mind will always provide more light for your continuing journey. We have much to learn. May we find the wisdom to continue the search.

Errors

JANUARY 20, 2010

Over the last several years, I have had the privilege of sharing my thoughts with you in the *Fayette Falcon*. I try to read the article before sending it to the Falcon. Usually, I read the article after writing it to proof for syntax, grammar, sentence structure and thought development. I also use the spell check to detect any misspelled words and grammar. Even after I've done all of this, I'll read an article after sending it to press and find some errors ... an "s" left off of a word or even an "a or an" left out here or there. I keep telling myself that I need to be a little more careful not to make these mistakes. But I inadvertently let it happen. Even after writing about "errors" and trying to follow my own advice, I'll bet you will find an error. Hope not!

You might be asking "Why are you bringing this to the attention of the reading public?" I guess I am trying to say to myself, "Be more careful!" "Be more thorough!" I'm trying to learn even in the winter years of my life that doing a careful and thorough job in anything I attempt is essential. It is obvious that an added reading of an article can provide a more acceptable product, but not necessarily perfect. It is not good to be sloppy!

Many of our mistakes in life are similar to mistakes in writing to which I have been making reference. There are various phrases that come to mind. "Too quick to act." "Not enough time spent in reflection." "Failure to review what we have done." These statements have far-reaching implications. Misplaced letters or misspelled or left out words may have little consequence as I often say, "in the span of eternity." Other mistakes may communicate ideas you did not intend or create an impression you regret. So it is helpful to be careful in evaluating the words and ideas you try to share with others. It is essential to be careful in what we say and do; for we just don't know what is in the mind of the beholder. It is difficult to take back whatever it may be once it has reached the hearing and seeing of others.

One might say it is important to be self-reflective. This is hard! Yet it is vital if we want to bring words of value or engage in actions of help to those around us.

I would say that it is essential to develop a style of relating to others where we avoid writing or saying or doing things that diminish our effectiveness. If at all possible, review the product for public discourse before sharing it with the public. If at all possible, develop a way of communicating where you are able to be an impartial observer to yourself. Take time to prepare yourself where you never rush into something without a pause and a look. Today may be the day to share your thoughts, but you may want tomorrow to come after a day of pondering and a look by someone who will be neutral. My final word is "don't be so careful that you become too hesitant and fail to be truthful."

A Glimpse or a Vision

JANUARY 27, 2010

"To have faith is to be sure of the things we hoped for and certain of the things we cannot see." [Hebrews 10:1] I'm sure that you have heard someone say, "Keep the faith baby." When someone says this to you, they are saying to hang on no matter what. Much of the energy for the living of these days comes from living today -- in the present -- knowing there is something truly good out there that we strongly believe in. There is something out there that we cannot see, but we know exists which gives us encouragement and empowers us to keep on keeping on. When we lack that something, we get caught in the routine of mere existence. When we have that something, we can fly with the eagles and run with the horses. Based on this description of faith, let me share the verbal portrait of two persons. One person is named Haze. The other person Clear.

Haze is engaged in living. On the surface, he appears to be in control of his life ... greatly admired by many people for his determination and accomplishment. Haze's religious life has deep roots. He lives more by his human experience than his faith perspective. Right -- most of the time anyway! He would strongly protest someone challenging his motives for helping others as self-serving. So the voice of God for Haze is nothing more than a muffled sound in the distance. The light of a new day that seems to lead him might be only the glimmering light of a distant star. He holds tightly to the sound of his own voice and the light of his own thoughts. He is challenged to deny himself and sacrifice himself for what he speaks of as a truthful happening. His strong words turn into shouts of outrage or whispers of untruth. He looks through a glass darkly.

Clear is also engaged in living. As he moves along the continuum of his life, he shows some of the same drive to find fulfillment as Haze. He is a religious person and takes his faith seriously. He is less prone to be entirely right about everything, but more prone to question himself at least about some things. His steps along his journey have been quite bold, but then at times uncertain. At one time, he came to a crossroad and there he met death. The faith he has had in Jesus Christ over the years became more real than it had ever been. He began to live not merely out of his own voice and the light of his own thoughts, but as he walked with the Lord in the light of His words. He had visions that burst on his sight. He began to see through the eyes of faith clarity that overwhelmed and humbled him.

Haze and Clear represent two world views ... two ways of looking at reality. One saw the world and protected himself, or claimed the world for himself and sought to control all that he could. The other saw the world as truly a gift from God and gave himself for it and to it. How do you see the world?

Do this in Remembrance!

APRIL 14, 2010

Several weeks ago, I took advantage of the touch of spring and spent some time in the yard. My wife and I find ourselves at this time of the year preparing the flower beds for spring planting. The weeds will be gone, and within several months, the beds will be covered with beautiful flowers.

Year in and year out over the fall and winter months, the flowers die and the beds become covered with weeds. The weeds have to be rooted up and the beds prepared for planting. When faced with this weeding, I yearn for the day when there will be no more weeds and the labor of preparation will not be required. I don't believe that such a day is in the stars for the future.

Our moral and spiritual life is that way. We wish we could wipe away all of the unsatisfactory in us where perfection would rise like a beautiful sunrise and the darkness of the night never come. But that not the case! We always seem to have to weed our lives of the destructive and unsavory elements; otherwise, the negative and the evil can take over like the weeds.

Benjamin Franklin was known for an exercise of self-improvement. He would make a list of all the virtues and evils of life. He then proceeded to work on them either by elimination of the evils or development of the virtues. He realized that this was a lifetime endeavor. He would never reach the place of completion. The Apostle Paul in the Bible, talks about the putting off of those evil things in us and putting on the new life of love, patience, generosity, forgiveness [and the list goes on and on]. Whatever way, the recognition that the garden of our life needs weeding regularly is important, very important.

There is a hymn that begins with the words, "Take time to be holy, speak oft with your Lord." Is this what we are talking about? More than likely! Maybe it is important to take advantage of the occasions when we can "walk with the Lord in the light of His word; for what a glory he sheds on our way."

A Twist on Wisdom

APRIL 21, 2010

Is wisdom a hallmark of aging? Before we try to answer this question, maybe we should take a stab at defining wisdom. I found this straightforward definition in a dictionary on the internet. "The ability to discern or judge what is true, right, or lasting insight." Let's start with these words. We might say that wisdom is "lasting insight" that defines reality apart from our personal prejudices and passions. Often, we allow our personal prejudices and passions to affect our decisions about life. The more we are inclined toward making decisions that exclusively serve "oneself," the more we will be removed from discerning what is true, right and lasting.

This idea on how we relate to others may be a variation on wisdom that brings a fresh thought. Several weeks ago, I was engaged in a conversation on the ways of another person. One thought led to another where I began reflecting on the wisdom of this person described as a clear and thorough thinker -- although he tended to begin with a personal perspective and sought to prove his position. This would not be considered a search for truth where wisdom would prevail. In the world of thought labels, both liberals and conservatives can be guilty of this judgment.

I then began to investigate the notion of wisdom in this context. Wisdom seeks to communicate. The position I have just described tends to pontificate rather than communicate. When we pontificate, however thorough and accurate we may think we are, we are encapsulated in our own "limited world" of looking out and letting nothing in. If one might describe a development toward wisdom, the next stage would be, "I am still right, but you have a right to your point of view." We are at least listening! I believe that maturity in wisdom comes when it is said, "You and I have our respective positions, and there may be value to what you are saying." We not only listen, but seek to understand and even assimilate; with such openness, we become able to explore new horizons.

The beauty of dealing with life in this way is we realize enduring relationships that bring enrichment to our life. The world becomes open with a fresh breeze and a new splendor. We are no longer an individual standing in our own wilderness, but part of a vibrant existence. People no longer become "things to be used" but "persons to be loved and enjoyed." [Martin Buber]

My Purpose for Living

MAY 5, 2010

At my age, death increasingly becomes part of life's scene for friends and acquaintances. My son-in law said to me several weeks ago after the death of a mutual friend, "I have not experienced the death of so many people as I did this last year." Our mutual friend was a healthy person in his mid-sixties; all indicators pointed toward a vigorous, healthy person. When death comes, depending on the circumstances, many questions are raised and statements made. He seemed vigorous -- this doesn't make sense! This must have been his time. He lived a full life. His wife said, "He will be alright, I'm the one that will have the struggle."

We have in the passage of death a crossroad where the path for those who have died in some ways is a mystery. In another way, it becomes the gift of eternity. The Apostle Paul writes, "For me, to live is Christ, to die is gain." In other words, Paul is saying that while I continue my earthly journey "I will live for Jesus a life that is true, bearing allegiance in all that I do." He was also saying, "Upon my death, I will embrace the life of eternity as Jesus spoke of: "A home not made with hands eternal in the heavens." On this side of the curtain of death, we can exclaim with the Apostle Paul, "O death where is thy sting; O grave where is thy victory; yes, thanks be to God who gives me the victory in Christ Jesus."

Paul lived his life with a sense of a close walk with God. He realized that he had not arrived, but pressed on to what he called his "high calling in Christ." We who are alive are encouraged, strongly encouraged to press on. I remember from my younger years two older men who lost their wives at the same time. One had a strong sense of God's purpose for his life; he moved through his grief and sought God's guidance for the living of his life as it continued to unfold. The other man lacked that sense of holy presence and found himself claimed by a downward spiral of despair and excessive indulgence in alcohol.

After the death of another, those who continue along this earthly journey have a choice. Do I indulge myself in a narrowing world of self interests or do I give God the opportunity to work the miracle of renewed living as I seek his will for my life? The only answer that makes sense is to find a life where "I am living for Jesus a life that is true, bearing allegiance in all that I do." Another way to say this is "claim a new direction beyond the present horizon."

A Turtle in the Road

MAY 12, 2010

My wife and I were riding along Collierville-Arlington Road. There was a turtle in the middle of the road, along the center line. My wife commented, "There is a turtle in the road." I responded with several thoughts. "If a car veered across the line, the turtle would be smashed. If the turtle proceeded across the road and wandered into the car's lane, the end would come. If the turtle ventured away from the car or stayed where it was, the turtle would survive. The turtle is in a highly precarious location in his journey across the road."

This observance of the turtle's venture has much to say about a person's life. Like the turtle, we can find ourselves choosing the middle of the road, the neutral zones in life with the notion of staying safe. Maybe the neutral zone would provide a safe place; but not necessarily so. Staying in the neutral zone and finding safety depends considerably on how others around us behave. If they choose to follow the rules of the road, staying in the neutral zone will provide security. Unfortunately, everybody doesn't follow the rules of the road. And it takes just a slight variation on the rules to create problems for innocent people who are trying to live safely.

Another way of looking at the "turtle in the middle of the road" is in terms of the phrase, "don't rock the boat." You know something is needed for the well-being of others, but to do something would mean you would have to act contrary to the will of the majority. So you don't say anything or do anything. You would find security for yourself from this position, but the current way of thinking and doing would continue to be devastating for others.

Jesus was by no means "a middle-of-the-road person." He said to the people of his day, "I have not come to destroy the law and the prophets, but to fulfill them." Leaders, both religious and political, show ways of distorting the laws of righteousness and justice; they usually do this for their personal benefit. Jesus couldn't stand by and witness these distortions without making a challenge. Had he just remained quiet -- that is, stayed in "the middle of the road," he may have lived to a ripe old age. Jesus did not only die on the cross merely to bring the gift of eternal life, he established a new order of truth and justice rooted and grounded in love. While he challenged the enemies of a righteous order, he was quick to encourage his listeners to "love their enemies." Jesus said to the rich young ruler, "You can gain a world of security for yourself, yet still lose your eternal salvation." [Paraphrase]

Finding the Better Way

AUGUST 4, 2010

Last week, I had to remove a Bradford pear tree after a large limb had blown down. If you have ever had to do this, you are familiar with the procedure. The final step is to have the stump removed. The outcome is a neat pile of wood chips. In my attempt to even out the ground, there was a nice assortment of wood chips that had to be picked up and discarded. I had to pick up the chips, one at a time and put them into the wheel barrel to be discarded. Then there was the transfer of the chips into the garbage container. At this point, I could have taken each chip, as I had collected them from the ground, and put the chips into the container. But I chose to act differently. I gathered as many as I could with two hands and dropped the collected bundle into the container. I reduced the time considerably by changing my method of transfer.

Well, Sam that's an interesting story; what is the point? I am reminded of my father who had the knack of figuring out the most effective way of doing something. He would often say, "If there is an easier way, I want to find it." By bundling up the wood chips with both hands, I was able to reduce the time of transfer considerably. As I mentioned, I could have repeated the earlier procedure and transferred the chips, one at a time. It worked that way. But something in my head told me there was an easier way and my mind went to work figuring it out.

This story shares a simple activity yet communicates a profound principle of life. More often than not, there is always a better, more effective way to engage life's tasks. I probably, thinking back, could have picked up the larger chips from the ground by bringing them together. I could have raked them up into a pile and picked up the pile. Why is it that we are so reluctant even to ask the question, "Is there a better way?" When we find a way to do something and become comfortable in the procedure, we usually don't want to change, even if someone says to us, "I can show you a better way." As a society over the years, we have taken a quantum leap into an easier and more effective lifestyle because we have asked the question, "Is there a better way?" And having asked the question, I found the answer.

Knowing Jesus Christ as the way, the truth and the life is a better way. When we codify Jesus into merely a religious way and become satisfied, we then lose Him as the better way. He is always encouraging us to realize we have not arrived, but are pressing on to a higher way. He not only encourages us, but gives us the strength to let go and let God be the author and finisher of our life.

Cleaning the Sore

AUGUST 18, 2010

"Cleaning the Sore" What a strange title for an article! I have shared my thoughts about the psychological health of a person and used the term, psychic pus. One person responded with the words, "that's a priceless description." Another person turned up her nose because of the disgusting thought the word, pus, communicates. The description, psychic pus, is an attempt to point out how damaging to the psychic system of resentment and anger toward others can become. Such conditions can fester in our psyche to the point of personal destruction. Yes, it is like a boil where the health of the body can only be realized by lancing the boil; in other words, removing the pus before applying healing medicine.

Our inner self is much like an infected area of the body when destructive psychic conditions take hold of us. These conditions have to be removed before any healing can happen. We can begin with resentment and anger, but the list will increase easily as we add greed, hostility, unbridled passions …. These conditions, among others, act like pus in a sore. The infection will spread and the psychic health of the person will be threatened. They have to be removed, expunged from the system.

The overwhelming message of Jesus Christ is to "deny one's self" and "think of others more than you do yourself." This call to move away from being self-centered to being other-centered is so important. When we are preoccupied with ourselves and other people hurt us or take advantage of us, we have a tendency to feel sorry for ourselves and mean-spirited toward others. This results in anger and hostility which are infectious conditions that can literally destroy us. When we are preoccupied with merely meeting our personal wants and this spills over into greed and uncontrolled passions, we can literally destroy ourselves and alienate others.

Merely removing the infection is not sufficient. We need to re-connect with our God who is the source of health and new life. I am reminded of a hymn that amplifies and expresses my thoughts. "Oh! For a closer walk with God, a calm and heavenly frame ... I hate the sins that made thee mourn and drove thee from my breast. The dearest idol I have known, What'er that idol be, Help me to tear it from thy throne, and worship only thee."

Drop It

SEPTEMBER 8, 2010

I was in conversation with someone the other day when the person said, "Well, we ought to drop it." [The implication was there is no need to pursue the matter under consideration.] I responded "Maybe, not drop it, rather set it aside for consideration later." As I reflect on this conversation, I thought the phrases "drop it" and "set it aside" provide an intriguing contrast in dealing with differences over issues.

Dropping something implies no further discussion or consideration of the issue. For all practical purposes, any further conversation would be of little or no value. And often when someone suggests "dropping it" this indicates the dead end has been reached. But we need to be sure that the dead end has been reached before giving up. We also need to be sure that we're not taking an action that we will regret in the future.

Setting something aside implies that, in time, there is the possibly, with a change in circumstances or attitude, the issue could be further pursued. In parliamentary procedure, this would be defined as "tabling an issue." We know that tabling an issue means putting it aside where it can be taken up in the future. I guess what I am suggesting is the importance of not being precipitous and dropping something that does not seem solvable today, but could effectively be dealt with in the future. So at times it becomes appropriate to set something aside for future consideration. Determining when this should be done is the crucial question! But the consideration should be kept on the table.

Thus far, my intention in writing these words is to encourage the reader to take a long view when engaged in dealing with circumstances and relationships before giving up. Often too much is at stake! For example, today the Israelis and Palestinians have resumed talking about settling their differences. They are taking their issues off the table and making another run at it. They desperately need to reach a settlement for the well-being of their people and a peaceful world. While this is a crucial one, there are many, many issues in life that should not be dropped with the idea there is no solution. For no solution often means no future; and no future results in a closed door to life. The joy of living is moving out of the shadows of the present into the sunshine of the future.

The Days after Christmas

DECEMBER 29, 2010

The days that followed the birth of Jesus were quite eventful. Rather than a trip home, it became a journey into the far country. Jesus' parents took him to the land where his forefathers had been slaves. This was the land out of which they had come by the mighty hand of God; from slavery to freedom. This former place of slavery for a time would be a place of protection. This place of protection would become the launching place for our Lord' preparation for life.

The words that come to mind are <u>protection and preparation</u>. As I have often said, "God has a purpose for all of us." First and foremost, we need to remember that we have been "created in the image of God to do the will of God." Remember the words about Mary when the shepherds and the wise men departed. While the wise men and the shepherds were going forth to glorify God, Mary pondered these things in her heart. As the nativity account is told, the Holy Spirit revealed to Mary the anointed role of the child she was carrying in her womb. Mary's [and Joseph's] role was to protect and prepare Jesus to be able to claim his anointed role. This trek to Egypt became a journey of protection. His return to Nazareth was to begin his years of preparation for God's calling.

CELEBRATING THE BIRTH OF CHRIST [THE BEGINNING OF NEW LIFE] UPON A NEW YEAR IS HELPFUL. This is the time of the year we are wrapping things up and getting ready for a new year. It seems entirely appropriate to be reminded of the gift of new life that comes with Advent and Christmas. We do not exist solely for a journey from birth to death into eternity. In the journey of faith, life is best lived as we stop along the way and engage life, rather than stay on the super highway from start to finish.

The future is always emerging with the invitation to participate in new and grand happenings. This is what Jesus Christ is about. Advent reminds us that we live at the threshold of new beginnings, not "old endings." Life should always be lived as if we are getting ready for a new trip. This does not mean that today is irrelevant. We are living out yesterday's preparations and getting ready for tomorrow's trip. The important thing is to be prepared to respond to whatever happens along the way. The trip is as much a part of life as the destination.

"Day is dying in the West -- Heaven is touching earth with rest ... Work and worship while the night sets her evening lamps alight through all the sky." We should not let the end of a life's cycle govern the way we live ... nor live as if the day were the mere prelude to night. Rather, recognize that beyond the night is always another day as fresh as the morning dew and inviting as the rising sun.

Latch onto the Affirmative

JANUARY 5, 2011

We are into another year! What is going to happen this year? How are we going to deal with what happens? The last century provided a song that may give us some guidance on how we might deal with these happenings this next year. "You've got to accentuate the positive ... Eliminate the negative ... And latch on to the affirmative ... Don't mess with Mister In-Between. You've to spread joy up to the maximum ... Baring gloom down to the minimum ... Have faith or pandemonium's ... Liable to walk upon the scene."

Is it fair to say that the world is divided mainly into two types of people: those who always see the glass half empty and those who see the glass half full? The half empty folks are people who fail to see the possibilities in life, particularly in the face of difficulties; they often overreact and make that which seems bad even worse. And then there are the folks who look at life through what is called rose colored glasses. Everything is going to be just fine, even in the worst of times; they pass over lightly some of the difficulties that require attention.

Does this mean we live in that the world of "Mister In-Between?" This song that came out of the last century suggests, not necessarily. "Accentuate the positive, eliminate the negative, and don't mess with Mister In-Between." It is true that there are times when everything is not going to turn out well. But it is also true that life is good and just. One of the significant notes of the Christian faith is captured in words, "For God so loved the world that he gave his only son; that whoever believes in him will not perish, but have everlasting life. Christ did not come into the world to condemn the world, but to save the world." Even beyond this noble thought about God's action in Christ there is resounding evidence in every corner of the earth that after a storm there is the calm; after a war there is peace. Christ strongly affirms this basic fabric of humanity's existence.

When we live in terms of the negatives, we allow deterioration of life and death to claim us. When we settle down as Mr. In-Between it seems to me that "time like an every rolling stream still bears us all away." The story of creation reads that after God had created the world, he look at His creation and said, "It is good." Much depends on how you see life. I see life as a sunrise, not a sunset. I see our existence not in terms of death, but life. I see a significant principle of life as growth not stagnation. I'm enriched with the words of the Apostle Paul, who wrote to the Romans, "O death where is thy sting, O grave where is thy victory; thanks be to God who gives us the victory in Christ." So, why not "eliminate the negative, and latch on to the affirmative and don't mess with Mister-In-Between."

This Moment in Time

FEBRUARY 16, 2011

"This Moment in Time" is that point in time when yesterday died and tomorrow began. I inadvertently said to someone "such a moment can be one of the most crucial times in your life." As I reflect on this thought, I ask myself the question, "What did you mean when you spoke those words?" What did I mean!

Maybe what I meant was that at any moment in time, we have the opportunity to seize truth. I am reminded of the lightening bug. When I was a boy, we would go out into the night to catch lightening bugs. Some call them fire flies. Unless the lightening bugs lit up, you could not see them in the dark. When they lit up, momentarily, this was the time to reach out and grab them. If you hesitated, you would miss the chance to catch the bug. Things happen to us, by us and around us that help us understand the past and serve as a springboard for the future. But too often, we miss grasping the opportunity and truth of the moment because we are so preoccupied with "passing time;" as to say, what is happening to me [and those around me] or what will my future be like.

So let me suggest that it's necessary to allow time to reflect upon and absorb what is happening to you and around you. When you do this, you are better able to claim your future and not just ride into the future. You not only claim your future, but you are able to discern what God is calling you to be and do with your life. Just holding onto the past is like driving with extremely dark glasses. Such glasses not only protect your eyes from the sun, but also prevent you from seeing clearly. If you are always planning for the future, you miss what is emerging in the present. Beyond our experiences and future dreams, much is happening to us and around us on the stage of life. Unless we grasp these happenings, we are like riding a fast horse, away from the past and into the future. It is like riding on a super highway observing remarkably little along the way. Never forget that "God is working his purpose out as years succeed to years." It is vital to be still and know that God is near and observe the mighty acts of God on the stage of life.

An Improvised Life

MARCH 8, 2011

Recently, I came across the title of a book that fascinated me. The title was, "An Improvised Life: A Memoir" by Alan Arkin. Alan Arkin is an actor that has appeared in over 80 films. He began his career in the Second City Improv comedy troupe in Chicago. The improv theatre creates a drama by taking a situation without a script and by relying on a group of actors to expand on that situation. Look up in a Thesaurus the word "improvised" and you find these synonyms: off the cuff, unrehearsed, spontaneous, unplanned.

We are often guided in our education to believe that the best life is one that is prepared, planned, rehearsed, clearly defined and deliberate. No doubt, it is advantageous to know where we are going in life

… to have goals and plans to achieve the goals. For sure, it is not wise to deal with life off the cuff/without any sense of what you are going to say or do next. We probably would say that no one would build a house this way, or plant a field or undertake a vital task without knowing what the issue is all about and what you are going to do.

May I explore with you that without the improvised as part of your scheme of living, you would be at a loss to the spontaneous. There would be no dreams shared. There would be no visions explored. The new and fresh, the rich and full in life would be lost. Our imagination would be imprisoned to the established structures and planned procedures. In actuality, the living Spirit, which blows through all of us, would find no place to stir the heart and engage the mind. Our tomorrows would be merely routines drawn on the drafting board rather than pictures formed by the brush of a living hand.

There is a place in this world for the improvised life! Don't forget that the most effective improvised life is the life that seeks with open eyes and attentive ears and searching hearts and attentive minds, yes, that seeks to claim the heights and depths of life. "This is my Father's world and to my listening ears, all nature sings and round me rings the music of the spheres." [verse 1, hymn, Maltbie Babcock, 1901]

Resurrection

APRIL 20, 2011

Next Sunday all over the world, Christians will be gathering to worship the risen Christ. The common theme will be that Jesus "died and was raised from the dead to set us free from sin and death." I believe that the declarations of the Christian Church spend much more time on "freedom from sin." I want to take time with you this week to reflect on the far-reaching meaning of freedom from death.

When I was about nine years old, I came down from my upstairs bedroom and stood outside of the kitchen where my mother and father were. I had just had what some might call a nightmare. I was overwhelmed with the notion that I would die someday and would never be again. This sense of not being is a frightening experience. Faith in Jesus Christ is supposed to bring us close to God who is loving and forgiving. With this sense of closeness, we are encouraged to believe that we have a life that will never die. With such a belief, we are able to overcome this horrible fear of not being some day. The belief that Jesus was raised from the dead gives us hope that when we died, we too will be raised from the dead.

But there is a profound meaning to this victory over death for our day-to-day living. I don't know if we realize that death has a choking effect on our daily life. We may be insecure about our existence and rely too much on material prosperity. When we become too involved with "me, myself and I," we become entombed in our own world. The tragedy here is that the beauty of life and the fresh winds of vitality come to us as we give of ourselves in love and care for others -- not as we live merely for ourselves. How often have we heard it is more blessed to give than to receive? Believe it or not, IT IS!

Jesus said to an extremely rich man one time, "You can gain the whole world and lose your soul." The need to please ourselves can drive us to use people for our own gain and pleasure. A Jewish philosopher, Martin Buber wrote, "We humans often love things and use people. We are challenged to love people and use things." In order for this to happen, we truly have to die to self before we can share in the resurrected life. Jesus also reminds us that a seed must fall into the ground and die before the plant can grow and flourish. So it is with our own lives; we must let those deadly passions for self die, so that the new life that God breathes into us will grow and flourish.

Easter is a splendid celebration of this possibility of new life that the risen Christ offers to all who believe. It is the recognition that we don't have to be afraid of not being some day. The Apostle Paul wrote, "Oh death where is thy sting, Oh grave, where is thy victory?

Thanks be to God who give us victory in Christ." Because He lives, we can not only face, but claim tomorrow.

2. View the Landscape

Our inner self, which is influenced by life experiences, frames what we "see" happening before us. At the same time, we require a holy/spiritual presence to claim the very best and to deal with the very worst in life. In this crucible of viewing, we short-change this perspective when we simply see death as part of passing time by natural phenomena and human behavior. Let us never forget that while death is happening, new life is emerging. How do we view this landscape with enhanced spectacles?

Endurance

Endurance is needed to overcome the adversities and difficulties of life. It also is needed to deal properly with the opportunities and blessings that we are granted. Much depends on the way we live our lives. To begin with, it is necessary to express thanksgiving for the gifts of love and hope. Love and hope provide us life and sustain us through our uncertainties. We might call love and hope the two sides of our security blanket. One would observe that merely being bound to our principles with no regard for the other person's principles becomes a flight to the death of life. Love and hope take us beyond ourselves to embrace the other; they take us off the road to death and put us on the road to life.

I have had to set impatience aside and allow time for life to develop. There needs to be a touch of laughter to realize vital hope, active love, and diminished sadness. We must never forget to believe in each other, work and play together, and yes, never give up. Believe me, our life then will be migrating progressively out of the sunset and into the sunrise.

Opportunities

"All the world is a stage and all the men and women merely players." [Shakespeare] While we play on the stage of history, events are occurring and changes are happening. Opportunities for new life and development are present in these events and changes. When we live for that of which we hope, we are sensitive and responsive to the events and changes that enable our hope. With open eyes, alert minds, and strong passions, shaped by empathy and compassion, we can discern a new and fresh approach. Then and only then will we clearly see the opportunities, not only for ourselves but also for others, in the events and changes occurring around us.

Blessings

All around are the manifestations of blessings, happenings in words and actions, that encourage us to claim hope over discouragement. Blessings bring happiness to the core of our being. I have come to realize that the recognition of blessings becomes the way of dealing with the negatives in life. The awareness of blessings gives us a spirit of thankfulness. Let the Advent Season, the announcement of new beginnings, come as a time of encouragement in the midst of uncertainties. After that, celebrate Christmas as the time when we recognize our blessings, rather than count our gifts. We are able then to be thankful to be alive and empowered to share our self [and our resources] with others. It is important to suggest that Christianity does not completely corner the market on a message of blessings – but it is the recognized flagship of this perspective; whatever our spiritual tradition, we can find those blessings that engender hope and acknowledge new life.

There is that flipside to the recognition of blessings. We must never stop with "Count your many blessings, name them one by one, see what God has done." I would suggest that we extend the recognition of our blessings by being a blessing to others -- that is, engage ourselves and share our resources with others. Memorial Day, a holiday on the calendar, calls for recognizing our blessings in terms of giving life. We then are encouraged to recognize also our existence in the essence of God; "for God so loved the world that he gave." We are told that God gave himself so that humankind could have life, abundantly. When the holy/eternal presence controls us, we give in order that others might have the abundant life. As one might say, we become conduits of God's love.

Rainbow in Victoria Falls, Livingston, Africa

A *rainbow* is a *blessed* sign of a *new day*. "All around us are the *manifestation* of *blessings*, happenings in *words* and *actions*, that *encourage* us to claim *hope* over discouragement." SBL

The Teethsavers Ministry

A dental hygiene program started by Dr. Jack Rudd.
Zambia, Africa

Becky caring for the children

There is the *flipside* to the *recognition* of *blessings*. I would suggest that we extend the *recognition* of our *blessings* by being a *blessing* to *others*.

SBL

When the *holy/eternal presence* controls us, we *give* in *order* that *others* might have the *abundant* life.

SBL

Sam assisting

Blessings

Over the weeks and months to come, I look forward to coming into your homes by way of the *Fayette Falcon*. It is my intention to share insights from my personal life and faith journey. I want you to give me some idea of subjects of interest to you. A question, a thought, whatever it may be could become the basis of an article.

I want to begin my conversations with you by introducing myself. I am a retired Presbyterian minister serving the Oakland Presbyterian Church. I believe that retirement is but another stage in our everlasting journey. One of the thoughts that shape my life is from a poem by Elizabeth Browning, "Rabbi Ben Ezra." A paraphrase of the quote is *"Grow old along with me, the best is yet to be, the last for which the first was meant."* These words by Browning suggest that we can maintain a positive attitude as we journey into the aging years of our life.

I have often heard that the difference is how we look at life. The hour glass is often used to define the perspective: half full or half empty! When we look at life half empty, we tend to measure life in terms of what we don't have or in terms of the problems and difficulties around us. When we look at life half full, we tend to think about the blessings and the possibilities. Over half a century ago, Norman Vincent Peale was known for his messages on positive thinking. In a way, we are talking about positive thinking.

True, it's hard to think positively when everything around seems negative. So there has to be some way in which we can direct our attention away from the negative. This does not mean we disregard the destructive conditions that produce our negative thinking. Negative thinking can destroy us. So we have to find something that will help us be aware of the positive in our life. Positive thinking builds us up.

Our blessings provide for us a way of dealing with the negative and building us up. Each Sunday during worship I provide a time to share our thanksgiving and share our concerns. I truly believe that when we "count our blessings, naming them one by one, we see what God has done." In recounting our blessings and expressing thanksgiving we place our life in the context of a creation of justice and love.

Another way to frame our life positively is to recognize the possibilities in our life. One of the phrases that I encourage people to remove from their conversations is, "that can't be done." My faith is God as revealed in Jesus Christ empowers me to recognize the possible in the face of what others would suggest being impossible.

My suggestion to you this day is to know that the "best is yet to be." The way to do this is to count your blessings and acknowledge your possibilities. Take a moment, make a list of both your blessings and your possibilities in your life. Reflect on this list to find a reinforcement of your inner self as you continue your journey.

After the Storm

FEBRUARY 7, 2008

WRITTEN AFTER THE KATRINA HURRICANE
IN SOUTH LOUISIANA AND MISSISSIPPI

This past week, a storm, a very destructive one, moved across this area. Human lives were lost and property destroyed. Many lives have been ripped apart by the destructive force of nature. Having the ability to keep on keeping on when our lives are disrupted in such a devastation is extremely important. One of the essential qualities of life is endurance in the face of the difficulties, roadblocks and barriers that threaten our lives.

We find that the early Christians were faced with many difficulties, roadblocks and barriers that endangered their lives. One of the prominent themes of the Apostle Paul was the importance of "keeping on keeping on" For him, endurance was more than just putting up with his situation, rather becoming more than a conqueror through Christ who loved him. In other words, facing and dealing with our trials in life produces stronger persons. We will never reach our destination, never reach our goal in life if we allow the difficulties or roadblocks or failures to cause us to give up and not "keep on keeping on."

We can't let the difficulties or the roadblocks or the failures of today stop our forward movement. We just have to find ways to deal with life. I am reminded of a person who was born without arms. He was a very bright person. Over a period of time, he learned to use a stick in his mouth to operate a computer. I find myself from time to time singing the song "We shall overcome, we shall overcome some day." Endurance requires the belief that we can overcome.

Two qualities are essential to endure the totality of life: wisdom and strength. The lack of wisdom [understanding] and strength are shown in a vacillating life, being tossed about, unable to make clear decisions. When we lack sufficient insight, understanding or knowledge we might have to go back to the drawing board. For me, as a Christian, the drawing board involves my relationship with God whom I consider to be the source of wisdom and strength. When we act decisively we become stronger. When we become stronger we act decisively.

We learn from athletics that to win the game, you need to know how to play the game. I have a grandson who runs the hurdles in track. I can see that the more he practices and learns the techniques, the easier it gets to execute the run. This is true about life. To "keep on keeping on" … "to overcome" … "to move ahead through thick and thin." For me, that requires walking with God in "the light of his way." When I choose to walk with God, I know that he is walking with me.

Looking out of the Window

FEBRUARY 25, 2008

I want to share a story to help us understand that each and every human being sees life somewhat differently. By seeing life differently, I am thinking about what we see and how we interpret life from where we look. I have chosen to call this story, "Looking Out of the Window."

This story is about two men in a hospital room. One of the men was in a bed right next to the window. The other man was in a bed on the other side of the room. The man next to the window verbally shared what he saw. His comments went something like this: "It sure is a joy to look out of the window each day. Down in the areas below the window there is a beautiful garden with a cherry tree in the middle. Around the tree are seasonal flowers. I don't know the names of the flowers, but they surely are beautiful. In the spring and summer, there is like a blanket of red around the tree. In the fall and before, the flowers are various shades of colors ~ purple and yellow. Throughout the year, the cherry tree is adorned with its bright green leaves and the beginning of flowers. These flowers are beautiful; they have a pinkish white cast to them. Unfortunately, the flowers don't stay on the tree as long as I would like. The flowers fall to the ground like a fresh snow. The tree keeps its leaves until fall comes. The leaves drop to the ground like the flowers, and there appears the bud that will provide this beautiful cycle once again." Of course, the man by the window did not say all of this at one time. Rather, he provided an ongoing description of what he saw each day as he looked out of the window.

The man across the room was envious of the man next to the window because all he could see was the open sky across from the window. He was actually a bit angry with the man by the window. In his own mind, he rather wished that the man at the window would die. Why? Of course, so he then could get his place and find such joy in seeing such beauty.

One day, the "man by the window" died. The man across the room was given the bed next to the window. The first thing he did was to look out of the window. What did he see? There was open space and a concrete floor -- nothing else. No tree manifesting the changing seasons or flowers providing a blanket of beauty at the base of the tree. True, the man who saw the tree and flowers had visualized something that was not there. But from the beauty of his inner self he was able to create a picture of enduring worth for himself while confined in ill health to that bed next to the window.

I learned a long time ago that "life is in the eye of the beholder." We can take the drab and destructive dimensions of life and live in the morose of our own misery. We can reach for the beautiful in life and transform the drab and destructive into a fuller and richer world.

'Twas a Miracle

APRIL 30, 2008

Yes, it was a miracle. Into the night, a cry was heard. It was the cry of a seven year old girl who had a severe pain in her head. Her name is Jennifer. The doctors diagnosed the source of her pain as a tumor in the center of her brain. It was inoperable. She had a short time to live. Jennifer's family was an integral part of the congregation I served. You can imagine this young family's pain became an integral part of their church family.

Her father did not accept the diagnosis as being final. While her parents took advantage of medical treatments, they turned to God in prayer, fasting and tithing; yes, tithing. To shorten this story, let me go to the outcome. Jennifer's tumor disappeared after a time. The doctors had no medical explanation for this happening. They even chose to use the word miracle to explain this outcome.

Jennifer was affected by the tumor. She would never be the stately beautiful and bright adult that she might have become. Over the years, her parents provided for her opportunities for learning and personal development that would give her skills to become a teacher's aide.

This miracle also had a far-reaching impact on the congregation. We became a more significant fellowship of care and giving. And over the years, nearly twenty, these people of God have grown in commitment to Christ, numbers and ministry.

Several years ago, I returned to the congregation for the 50th anniversary celebration. Jennifer, in her twenties, approached me, wrapped her arms around my waist and said, "Sam, I love you."

I imagine that when asking parents, "What wishes would you have for your children?" ... their response might include physical health and attractiveness and an alert mind. Jennifer did not have either of these attributes from society's measurements. What she did have was the gift of unconditional love. When we allow ourselves a moment of honesty we would acknowledge that the gift of love is more precious than being attractive or mentally enriched. I am reminded of the Apostle Paul's words, "Now abide faith, hope and love, but the greatest of these is love." We must remind ourselves of the words, "God is love." I realized that Jennifer's hug brought me close to the strong embrace of God.

Yes, it was a miracle. A miracle turns us away from our human power and control and enables to us to realize the all-embracing presence of God. To God be the glory, great things he hath done.

P.S. Jennifer died in 2010. Restoration and the opportunity for continued life I believe, along with Jesus, is a gift of God to show forth God's glory and fulfill God's purpose. Jennifer showed forth God's glorious love and fulfilled her God-given purpose in life. "The strife is o'er, the battle done, the victory of life is won."

You Never Know

JUNE 3, 2008

Several weeks ago, the news coverage was much about Senator Edward Kenney's illness. One of the reasons his illness is on my mind is that he is just one year older than I am. A year ago, he was moving about with an apparent sense of well-being and no idea of the impending finality of his life. Within a short time, a malignant brain tumor has developed that is described as fast growing. I am reminded of a hymn, "Time like an ever rolling stream bears all its sons away ...." We may enjoy robust health today, but tomorrow we do not know. So the question we ask is, "How must we live today with the uncertainty of tomorrow?"

Should we adopt the hedonistic attitude expressed in the words, "Let's eat, drink and be merry for tomorrow we may die?" In other words, let's just enjoy life, get the most out of it for ourselves, with little regard for others, except maybe our immediate family, for death will come." No doubt, death is coming to all of us, some time or another. But is this "self-consuming" approach to life proper, whether we have a short or long fuse left? There may be a number of folks who believe that this would be the approach, but I personally don't think so.

There is tremendous pleasure derived from living a life that seeks to satisfy one's own personal interests, desires and pleasures. Yet much can be realized in letting oneself become a conduit of eternal love. I've come to the conclusion that it doesn't have to be one way or the other way, but can be both ways. When I was a boy, I learned what we called in the church, The Catechism. One of the questions asked was "What is man's chief end?" The answer was, "Man's [and woman's] chief end is to glorify God and enjoy Him forever." I believe that God has created us to appreciate our many benefits and blessings. One of the most significant aspects of enjoying our blessings and benefits is to share them with others. Is it possible that the people who realize the most from life are those who give the most to life!

None of us knows the day, the time or the place when the breath will leave our human body and the end to this earthly journey will come. But we all know it will come ~ maybe tomorrow, next year, ten years from now or with the twinkling of the eye. Jesus would say, "Don't worry about your life's needs or tomorrow; God provides for you today and tomorrow." Have faith and live in love. Care a big bit today! Share a big bit today! And when the sun begins to set, give thanks to God for the breath of life and expressions of love. You won't regret it!

Endurance

JUNE 24, 2008

Nature is raising its mighty hand of havoc on the planet earth; we are experiencing on a regular basis fires, floods, tornadoes, earthquakes ... and along with these, the sense of helplessness. The stark realities of illness, accidents, and death impact our lives on a fairly regular basis and along with these, a sense of helplessness. For a major portion of earth's population, poverty, war and oppression make them vulnerable to any opportunity of a real new day or a breaking dawn of hope.

In such a world, it is difficult to endure, in other words to "keep on keeping on". The tendency when things are getting really bad is to resign ourselves to the situation and lose confidence.

Jesus entered the world of his day where he saw the people in considerable distress. He was a person who showed deep empathy for the people of his day whom he described as helpless and worried. He offered them a package of help and hope. This package includes insights into living, relief from their physical [and emotional illnesses] and the announcement of a new day.

This package of help and hope INVOLVED GETTING RIGHT WITH GOD. As the Apostle Paul describes in his letter to the Roman Christians, we find this simple formula: "getting right with God" results in peace with God.

It sounds so simple: "Get right with God." But we always and forever find the drama of human life puzzling by asking the question, "Why do good people suffer?" The problem with such a question is we begin with ourselves and our own righteousness. Let me suggest that this is the wrong starting place ~ our own goodness. For we learn from scripture [in a familiar word] that "all have sinned and fallen short of the glory of God."

The Apostle Paul challenges us to change the way we look at life. Our renewed relationship with God through faith in Jesus Christ enables us to boast in our troubles [a rather unique way of looking at life, when we usually <u>complain</u> about our <u>troubles</u>, and boast only in our <u>successes</u>]. Why boast in troubles? Troubles, through our faith in God, can produce endurance which results in a hope that will sustain us. We get up and move ahead to live another day!

We no longer are relying on ourselves, but on a self where we have a new hope ... a hope based on God's love for us, not our own strength -- not our own wisdom and not on the good things happening in the world -- rather, God's love. We affirm over and over again in the quicksand of our troubles that "nothing can separate me from the love of God." I will overcome ... I will overcome .... Yes, "there are things I do, I shouldn't do and thoughts I think I shouldn't think. Who will deliver me from this body of death? Thanks be to God who gives me the victory through Jesus Christ." Endurance is an essential dynamic of our life. Never give up. Keep hope alive. Press on. The sunrise of tomorrow will surely come.

An Old Body ~ A Young Person

AUGUST 13, 2008

We find somewhere in the New Testament of the Bible the words, "While the outward person is growing old, the inward person is being renewed day by day." [paraphrased] This year, I reached my 75th year. No doubt, the body is no longer young, but I have often said that I am a young person in an old body. John Quincy Adams, one of our founding fathers, was asked, "How are you John?" He responded by saying, "This old house of mine is showing the wear of time. The shingles are falling off. The house needs painting. But John Quincy Adams is fine." And I am reminded of words in Browning's writing, Rabbi Ben Ezra, "Grow old along with me, the best is yet to be; the last for which the first was meant." Yes, I truly believe that we can continue to be a "young person" as the body continues to age. I want to share a few thoughts that might inspire you into being a "young at heart" thinker.

The first thought is that we have to <u>realize a new birth of life in spite of the aging process</u>. Have you ever tried to promote a new idea or way of doing something and before you get the idea out someone says, "I don't care for that!" or "I don't believe that will work!" These statements are what I call "door shutters to the future." We become possibility people if we are able to open doors into tomorrow. I am reminded of the song {The Impossible Dream} from "Man of La-Mancha". *"To dream the impossible dream ... To run where the brave dare not go ... To right the unrightable wrong ... This is my quest ... No matter how hopeless ... no matter how far."* These selected words from the song give us a sense of the young heart hampered by nothing ... claimed by everything. Yes, a new birth [and burst] of life is quite visible.

The second thought is that we have to <u>realize that the prevalent perspectives of life today won't cut it</u>. Another song comes to my mind: "Young At Heart." Some of the words shape this thought: "Don't you know that it's worth every treasure on earth ... To be young at heart ... For as rich as you are its much better by far ... To be young at heart." <u>Much of what we do today is motivated by creating "treasures on earth."</u> Maybe, it would be far better growing a heart of spiritual treasures [love, joy, peace, justice, kindness, forbearance], than to building a vault of earthly treasures and comforts. Jesus had much to say about this: "Seek first the kingdom of God and his righteousness and all these other things will be added ... you can gain the whole world and lose your soul." Or you can set yourself apart, find a challenge for self-giving and be renewed.

The third thought that comes to mind is also captured in the song, "Young At Heart." "Fairy tales can come true, it can happen to you if you're young at heart. For its hard, you will find, to be narrow of mind ... If you're young at heart." <u>We certainly don't want our hearts to shrivel up as our bodies wrinkle up</u>. A young person does not necessarily have a young heart. It is how we see it. "To the man who has a hammer," Mark Twain wrote, "Every problem looks like a nail." A young heart is an open heart that refuses to be controlled by the world of "me, myself and mine" but rather the universe of God's unconditional love and unfolding possibilities.

An Uncertain Tomorrow

AUGUST 20, 2008

A husband and wife left yesterday for Houston, Texas. They left three children at home with family and friends while they took this journey. This is a true story, but for the sake of anonymity I am going to refer to them as Bill and June. Bill has a cancerous growth in his tongue. This trip to the hospital for surgery will be his second effort to conquer this life-threatening condition. Not too many months ago, he had surgery with the belief that all would be well. This time, they go with the same expectation that "all will be well." I asked June what they might expect. She responded with the words, "We are hopeful, but we may be gone for several weeks."

After speaking with June before they left, I realized that this family is the age of my daughter's family: a son in college, a daughter in high school and the youngest in middle school. What would I be thinking and feeling if this were my family? Uncertainty! Hope! We never know the length of time we have upon this earth. But when a threatening disease has a grip on our body, we begin to think more in terms of shorter than longer. We recognize quickly that life may change more drastically, sooner than later. Yes, and there will be many adjustments to be made. But for now we hold on with hope that tomorrow will be a good day and that we will, yes, we will, enjoy a normal life for a time.

Living in hope does not mean that we fail to prepare for what may be over the horizon. In actuality, the best way to live in hope is to prepare ourselves for what the future may hold. When we are prepared, I believe we will rid ourselves of those anxieties that tend to cripple us along the way. Freedom from such anxieties allows us to live each moment, each day with a certain joy that flows out of a reverence for life. My thought would be that "the realized richness of each moment gives shape to the splendor of tomorrow."

The Apostle Paul wrote in one of his many letters the words, "Now abide faith, hope and love, but the greatest of these is love." As I watched this family over the last 10 years, there was never a day when Bill was not spending some time with his children. The lasting bond formed in these activities of love will give the family the strength it needs to press on in the face of evident uncertainty … but they will press on with hope, looking to share the rich moments that they will have in the tomorrows of their lives, as they did in the past.

We might say that it is important never to forget that the hope of tomorrow is built on the love of today ... our love for each other realized in the loving embrace of God.

Security at its Best

OCTOBER 15, 2008

There is a character in the comic strip *Peanuts*; his name is Linus. Linus walks around holding a blanket. He won't let the blanket out of his hands. This blanket has come to be known as his security piece. Whenever someone holds onto something for dear life we often say that this object is his or her Linus blanket. Of course, we know that "whatever it may be" does not have to be merely a blanket. It can be anything.

Possibly the best way to explore this notion of a security blanket is to put our mind in free association to think of all the things people use to promote security for their lives. What is it that you hold onto, possess so strongly, that if you lost it or it was taken away from you the uncertainty shakes would overwhelm you? Let me suggest several "things" in which we often hold onto for our security. Money! Possessions! Status! Position! Associations! Even People! We may have a tendency to hold onto any one of these things to give us confidence or well-being. If we have depended on anyone of these or something else to build our confidence, and we lose it, we acquire the deep frustration shakes.

I am reminded of the scripture verse that reads "Our help is in the name of the Lord who made heaven and earth…he that kept us will not falter." Other words from scripture that come to mind are found in the 23rd Psalm. "Though I walk through the valley of the shadow of death, I will not be afraid, for God is with me."

We are living in a time of much uncertainty. The financial world, while not crumbling, is shaky. The ability to take care of ourselves is being challenged. What should we do? Maybe it is time to stop relying on the "things of this world" [and even the people] and place our trust, truly place our trust, in the creator of this world. Please remember that "God so loved the world that he gave his only son, that whoever believes in Him will not perish but have eternal life."

Thoughts for Today's Living

NOVEMBER 5, 2008

We are living in uncertain times! Most of us remember the words of President Roosevelt when he said, "The only thing we have to fear is fear itself!" I wrote an article several weeks ago entitled "My Linus Blanket." In this article, I pointed out that we humans have our Linus Blankets, so to speak, our security blankets, those things and people and established ways we hold on to give our life stability and value.

We are reminded of Jesus' words that we are not to "lay up for ourselves treasures on earth where moth and rust consume, where thieves break in and steal, but lay up treasures in heaven." When our trust is entirely in things and even the people of this world, when the tsunamis of life overwhelm us, we stand helpless at the gates of material and economic ruins. We hear those assuring words, "Our help is in the name of the Lord, who made heaven and earth."

The Apostle Paul wrote a number of letters to the churches he started. These letters are found in the Bible. One of the letters he wrote was to a church in Philippi whose security was threatened. In the face of such uncertainty, Paul encouraged them to remember their union with Christ who died so they might have a more abundant life. Several other guiding thoughts were offered. Don't worry, but pray to God remembering his many blessings. Focus your thoughts on the "good things that deserve praise." When we approach life with these thoughts in mind, we come to realize a secure life. Regardless of the uncertainties around us, the stabilizing peace God has given to us in Christ brings certain calm over our life.

One other suggestion jumped out at me. And this suggestion has to do with our attitude. The word Paul used to describe the attitude which we have is the word, gentle. Gentleness is born out of a secure life. Gentleness brings calm to our life. Over the last weeks since reading Paul's words, I have engaged in the practice of gentleness. What a glorious day it is when your life is controlled by kindness, tenderness and longsuffering -- characteristics that describe the shape of gentleness.

The Days Have Come

DECEMBER 24, 2008

The angels and popular hymn bring to mind the announcement of the birth of the Christ child, "The hopes and fears of all the years are met in this child tonight." Tradition had affirmed him with the words, "For unto you a child is born, a son is given and he shall be called Wonderful, Counselor, the mighty King, the everlasting Father, the Prince of Peace." The Jewish people lived their lives in anticipation that God would send a Messiah to deliver them from their human oppression.

They were energized by the belief that God had not forsaken them, and that someday their lives would be better. When Jesus emerged out of the cocoon of his young adult years and was recognized as the one who would bring that better day, the story of his birth was exulted. Hear the angels, "Behold: I bring you good tidings of great joy for unto you is born this day in the city of David, a Savior." So as we celebrate Christmas this year let us not forget God's message of "a better day." And when the better day comes, let us not forget to give praise to our God and give thanks for that better day.

I am thinking about Christmas morning [this is the time when we as a family open our gifts]. In some ways, we often become so engrossed with the gifts we receive that we forget to acknowledge the giver. We not only become engrossed with the gift, but also with the value of the gift to us.

Maybe this year with all that is happening in the world, and in the face of our own personal situation, we may need to step away from how many gifts we have received ... or even what we have received. We may need to think about what life should be all about ~ joy and peace and love.

For fear of being trite, I would like to suggest several things. Could it be that the family that gathers to share the gifts is far more valuable than the gifts? Could it be that the freedom to play and laugh and speak our peace is far more important than all of the material benefits of our modern society? Could it be that the opportunity to share our resources to help others is far more needed than storing our resources for our future security?

Yes, Christmas Day has come! It has come not only to gather around a table of bounty. It has come not only to see how many gifts we have received or can give. It has come to remind us that with the birth of the Christ child, "the hopes and fears of all the years have been framed in the shape of joy and peace and love." We must always remember that regardless of how awful it may get, how difficult the times may become, or how little we have that tomorrow is a new day. It is not just a new day, but it is always the first day of a new life because "unto us a child was born, a son given, and his name will always be called Wonderful Counselor, the mighty king, the Everlasting Father, the Prince of Peace."

A Focused Approach to Life

MARCH 4, 2009

I enjoy taking pictures. One of the neat things about picture-taking with a digital camera is you can use the computer to enhance the pictures. There is one manipulation that can be made that helps with brightness. At one end of the spectrum, there is the word, darker, at the other end, the word, brighter. If you move the marker to either extreme, the whole picture is wiped out. At the dark end, the picture become fully dark and you can't see any of the details in the picture. At the light end, the picture becomes quite light, and you have lost all of the details in the picture.

In other words, there is no picture at either extreme. The picture at both ends is obliterated. The variations and details of the picture are lost. The vibrancy and shades no longer exist. We come to realize that both ends of the spectrum are the same. What was a picture at one time no longer exists.

My thoughts began to apply this exercise to the human scene. The words conservative and liberal came to mind. And I placed the conservative at one end, for discussion sake, the bright end. I placed the liberal at the dark end. (There is nothing significant about either end for the sake of this illustration). The significant insight is that both positions are lost in the maze of nothingness when lived at the extremes. Both have lost the variations and details of creative thought and action. Both have lost the vibrancy and shades of the truth which are necessary for effective life. The sad thing about adhering rigidly to principles, whether they be conservative or liberal, is truth and understanding are often lost in the hodgepodge of emotive thinking. We find ourselves in the night where we tend to stumble around, or we find ourselves in the hot, blinding sun where we can't see the path before us.

I am reminded of the words of an elder statesman in the mid-20th century. This statesman would say that the way to deal with problems and issues is to recognize the right detail may not be my way. He would suggest there is another area that comes from exploring the variations and details, seeing the vibrancy and shades and realizing a different and more excellent way. Again, let me point out that he would say that this new scheme is not my way or your situation -- not even a compromise of the two ways, but something that takes us above and beyond where we never intended to go or be. One might conclude it would be a new way born in the crucible that blends openness, exploration and mutual respect. Truly, this would be a serendipity and discovery moment.

The Reality of a Dream

APRIL 22, 2009

Jesus said, "I have come to give you life, abundant life." I imagine that not one person reading this article would abandon their desire for an abundant life. Of course, we would ask, "What is an abundant life?" I would answer, "The abundant life is different things to different people." For some, it might mean a luxurious house and all the money you needed to live in that luxury. For others, it might mean a well in their village where they could get fresh water. The difference in lifestyles throughout the world is quite striking, and hence, the "dreams of a better time" are equally striking.

One of the goals of the Founding Fathers of this nation was the realization of life, liberty and the pursuit of happiness; this would not only be in the grasp -- but a reality for all people. This is something people of justice and compassion want, not only for themselves, but for all people wherever they may live on this planet earth.

I believe that my Lord, Jesus had a dream. This dream was that all God's people, all the peoples of the world, some day would have the abundant life. When Jesus set out on his ministry, he quoted the prophet Isaiah, *"The Spirit of the Lord is upon me to set the captive free, hold up the broken hearted, heal the sick, give sight to the blind, help the lame walk, and tell the good news about God's loving presence in the world."* [paraphrase] He knew that this could happen when our broken relationship with God was put back together. He believed that the outcome of a new day with God would be a loving chord around this struggling world that brings a balm that would make the wounded whole, not just well.

The problem with all of us is that neither the big house nor the cup of water provides the abundant life. In the grander scheme of life, the "cup of water" produced by a new well in an African village comes closer to bringing the joy of living than does the luxurious house. The leper healed by Jesus was joyous because his body had been healed beyond imagination. But when he realized that this was an action of God's abiding love and the unfolding embrace of God, he experienced the fullness of his joy. At such a moment of joy, he knew the abundant life. Whatever it is that brings comfort or healing to us, we only understand the fullness of life when we give thanks to God for the blessings of life and live out of this thanksgiving by becoming a blessing to others. <u>Then we come to know the abundant life fully</u>.

After the Fact

JULY 8, 2009

We celebrated Independence Day this last weekend. Were you part of a family gathering? Did you participate in a community gathering with fireworks and all? I will bet you and the kids had a bag full of assorted fireworks that kept the neighbors awake into the night! Whatever you did and wherever you were, I'll bet you had a fantastic time.

Fireworks, flags, and patriotic music give us an emotional surge. We are put in touch with the incomprehensible reality of the expansive freedoms that we have, namely, freedom of religion, freedom of speech, freedom from want, freedom from fear. But we come to realize that such freedoms, enjoyed by all, require mutual respect by all people and for all people. When I choose to claim these freedoms for myself with little or no respect for others, I help create a climate that even diminishes my opportunity to enjoy the freedoms.

Have you ever asked yourself the question, "With all of the freedom that we have, why is it there is so much destructive activity in this nation?" Reinhold Niebuhr, a theologian of the mid-20th century, wrote that "the reason we have the law is because of the sinfulness of man." In a "Brief Statement of Belief" [1963] of the Presbyterian Church, sin is defined as pride and despair. As we reflect on freedom, let's focus on pride.

Pride, expressed in arrogance, drives us to improve our own freedoms while diminishing the freedoms of others. This lack of mutuality creates the climate of destructive behavior that leads to fear and creates want. The outcome is that "we all lose."

The sin of pride is subtle. Pride drives us to destructive behavior as we seek to accumulate possessions and power for our personal enhancement. Pride also pushes us into the realm of self-righteousness. Simply speaking, the slogan of the self-righteous is "I am always right, you are always wrong." This slogan controls the chambers of government and the sanctuaries of the church. With such a climate, it is difficult to find the way and the truth that would facilitate freedom from fear and want for all people. The appeal of Jesus came in the words, "Deny yourself, take up your cross, and follow my way of unconditional love." "Love one another as I have loved you."

Blessings

"There shall be showers of blessings; this is the promise of love; there shall be seasons refreshing, sent from the Savior above … showers of blessing … showers of blessing we need. Mercy-drops round us are falling. But for the showers we plead." These words from a gospel song give a bent to life that is often overlooked.

So much doom and gloom. So much self-serving! People fail to rejoice when the rain falls and grumble when the sun shines. We just can't seem to be satisfied. Yet all around us there are showers of blessings. God's gift of Jesus Christ is a blessing of irrefutable wonder. This gift of love gives awareness to all the blessings that provide us with life and hope and joy. Yes, life in the face of death … hopes in the face of doom … joy in the face of sorrow.

You see folks, our faith in Jesus brings happiness and joy. We should be shouting from the highest mountain the glory of the Lord. I don't understand why some people stay away from worship Sunday in and Sunday out; worship is an opportunity to share our happiness with others and praise God for his goodness. I don't understand why we don't come into the house of the Lord with bells on our shoes and a tambourine in our hand. We go along from day to day, take everything for granted, with little appreciation when we have been so blessed.

It is wonderful when we come to realize that we are blessed. "Every time I hear a new born baby cry … or touch a leaf … or see the sky I know why I believe." There are many ways we can define happiness: the birth of a child … a stable family … a long and prosperous life with someone. When we are blessed, we realize a feeling of self worth and a sense of accomplishment. But most of, all the awareness that we have been truly blessed by God.

God takes us further into the broader realm of human experiences. Jesus tells us that we can be happy [yes, blessed] even when we sorrow, because we will find comfort. We can be happy when we are down and out, because God will give us assurance of a better day. We can be happy even when life does not always deal us a so-called winning hand, because God will give us the strength to overcome.

I have a recording of a "Wonderful World" sung by Louis Armstrong. Some of the words are "The colors of the rainbow so pretty in the sky; are also on the faces of people going by. I see friends shaking hands saying 'how do you do.' They're really saying I love you. And I think to myself what a wonderful world."

The real beauty of recognizing our blessings is that we are thankful to be alive; this is truly a wonderful world. We realized a life of happiness. We worship a wonderful God. We have a wonderful friend in Jesus. We look for the opportunities to be wonderfully caring people. "And I think to myself, what a wonderful world."

Return ~ Stay ~ Go

OCTOBER 28, 2009

Jesus came to Jericho, a town south of Jerusalem. He was approached by a blind beggar, Bartimaeus. This blind beggar shouted out, "Jesus, Son of David, have mercy on me!" He shouted out a second time. Jesus responded, "Call him here." They called him. "Take heart; get up, he is calling you," he heard, He sprang up and went to Jesus. Then Jesus said, "What do you want me to do?" "Let me see again." Then Jesus said to him, "Go; your faith has made you well."

Bartimaeus was frozen in time. His lack of sight placed significant limitations on what he could do and where he could go. His personal freedom was restricted. He found himself to be overly dependent on others for his mere existence. The ability to see would give him, at least, the potential to frame a new life for himself. This cry for mercy was a cry to have this burden of blindness removed where he would realize the joy of seeing once again.

Before I go any further, I would like to make a suggestion. We can see with our physical eyes, and yet not see life as it really is. Our knotted conscience, our distorted world view, even our value system can restrict our life. The tragedy here is that we are far more blind when we have our physical sight and lack clarity than we are when we are unable to actually see.

The title of this article is "Return~Stay~Go!" This man could have returned to his life prior to blindness. We can never return to life, as it was, for so much has happened during the interim. We need to know and understand the changes to continue our journey. We surely don't want to stay in the darkness of our present life; other-wise, we wouldn't be calling for relief. The only way is to go forward as did Bartimaeus.

Having established the need for sight and the path we should take, what is it that sets us on this quest? We need to be aware we are blind. We furthermore want to be released from this restricted life. There is the belief we can be healed. Finally, we can stay where we are and merely depend on others to help us. As did the blind man, we have to get up and take the initiative; and when it happens, claim the opportunity for this new life.

Look Beyond

NOVEMBER 4, 2009

I visited with someone the other day. This person, a teenager, had gotten himself into some difficulty and had to spend some time in a learning situation apart from his routine. My advice to him was to look beyond and in the meantime, be responsible in his present situation.

From time to time, we find ourselves in situations that are uncertain or unpleasant. We may not be sure about what our immediate future will bring. We may be faced with conditions that possibly would be unkind to us. We can operate out of fear or frustration and consequently react quite negatively. Of course, the outcome of negative behavior is eventual destruction to you.

There are other alternatives couched in the belief that the outcome, regardless of how gloomy it presently is, will be good. I am repeatedly reminded of the words in scripture, "Be still and know that God is near." Jesus was on the mountain with several of his disciples. He was anticipating his death on the cross. This was not the best of times for Jesus. He was transfigured, or lifted up and was able to see beyond the cross to his resurrection. Because of this larger and more positive vision of life, he was able to endure the cross, bear the pain and become more than a conqueror. In other words, he was able to "Be still and know that God was truly present with him." A thought that might be helpful comes to mind: be still, take a breath and envision an acceptable outcome.

Much of our ability to live through hard times (the not so certain times, the disappointing times) is the awareness that God has the whole world in his hands; yes, you and me in his hands. In whatever time our destiny is played out, we know our life is of value. The Apostle Paul wrote about life and death: things past, present and future and in which nothing can separate us from the love of God.

Nearly ten years ago, I had bypass surgery. As I prepared to go to the operating room, I was asked, "How do you feel?" I responded, "I feel good. I have a good doctor. I am in the hands of a good team. My family loves me and is praying for me. And most of all, I am in God's hands and he continues to claim me." Some ten years hence, I know God is working his purpose out as years succeed to years. Remember the words of Dorothy in "The Wizard of Oz, "Somewhere, over the rainbow, way up high. There's a land that I heard of once in a lullaby. Somewhere, over the rainbow, skies are blue. And the dreams that you dare to dream really do come true." Thanks are to God who gives us victory in both life and death.

What it Would be Like

NOVEMBER 18, 2009

This last week, I was pulling out of my driveway in my car. I noticed that my neighbor was walking without his dog. Usually every morning, I would see John walking his dog. I stopped, rolled down my window and asked, "Where is your dog?" John responded, "He died!" From the look on his face, it was obvious that the dog's death was quite painful. John went on to tell me about his dog. I think he called his dog by name, Mark. Mark was 17 years old. The reference to his dog by name defined this relationship.

He proceeded to share with me the details of Mark's death. He said, "I don't have children, but I can imagine what it would mean to lose a child." This was quite a revealing statement. John and Mark had bonded like parent and child. He was experiencing that sense of loss that a parent might feel. I have two children and both have grown to adulthood and are living full lives. I have not lost a child in death, but as a pastor, I have walked with a number of families who have given their child up to death. The pain is deep because it is like losing a part of you. John felt as if he had lost a part of himself when his dog died. I saw a tear forming below his eyelid.

I went on to say, "Are you going to get another dog?" His response was, "Oh, no! This is my third dog to grow old and die." As he talked about his dogs, he spoke of each one by name. He did not want to go through this experience again. Maybe he will. Maybe he won't.

I told my wife that my article this week was going to be about my conversation with John and the death of his dog, Mark. She then mused out loud about what I might say. There is a song we teach children, "Friends, friends I have some friends I love. I help my friends, and they help me. I love my friends, and they love me." Our children become the object of our affections. A great deal of our life is invested in loving our children. We nurture them along. They do become our friends! Parents and children can reach adulthood and remain friends for a lifetime.

In many ways, our pets become much like a friend. It's not just a one-way relationship. As we take a young animal and care for it, giving it affection and love, this dependent relationship can realize a frame of mutuality much like parent and child. Thank God for our animal friends.

Keeping Hope Alive

DECEMBER 23, 2009

As we approach Christmas, we will hear over and over again in melodic sound, "The hopes and fears of all the years are met in thee tonight". Of course, these are the words attributed to the angels as they announced the birth of Jesus.

How do we keep hope alive? We keep hope alive by living in terms of that for which we hope ... not in terms of the destructive and debilitating forces around us and often inside of us. I want to share some thoughts about how we keep hope alive.

Be about the business of keeping hope alive by being engaged in life to "rescue the perishing, care for the dying, snatch them in pity from sin and the grave. Weep o'er the erring one, lift up the fallen. Tell them of Jesus the mighty to save." Jesus kept hope alive for the people of his day by doing this very thing. As we walk with the Lord in the light of his word and live as a conduit of his love, hope will live in us and through us.

Be about the business of keeping hope alive by really being co-creators with God in the care of his creation … all inclusive, man and beast, land and sea and sky. One of the significant themes today is a call to care for this all-inclusive world.

Be about the business of keeping hope alive by remembering that the church is the body of Christ and we look to him for our sense of destiny and our way for living … our time together in worship should always be a hallelujah day.

Remember God is working his purposes out. Keep hope alive! Share a cup of water with the thirsty. Provide clothing to the naked. Supply strength to the weak. Bring news for those lost in despair. Participate in the actions of justice for all of creation. You see, as we give hope to others, we keep hope alive for ourselves. We don't want to lose it. We don't want to possess it too tightly. We need to share "this new life," otherwise we will lose it. Keep hope alive!

Give Time

MAY 26, 2010

Do you ever get impatient for something to happen before its time? I bought three blockbuster roses about a month ago. About a week ago, all of the plants had gone through the early blossoming stage. I noticed that one of the plants was giving forth new sprouts. The second looked fantastic with no yellow leaves, but no new sprouts. The third was downright puny. I replaced the third one. The second one is showing marginal signs of growth and health. My wife tells me that I need to be patient and give it time to develop its root system and begin to show evidence of growth. I said, "Well, I'll give it a little more time; I have several more months to exchange it."

This review of my gardening is a parody on human life. In the book of Ecclesiastes in the Bible, we read, "Everything that happens in the world happens at the time God chooses ... A time for birth and a time for death ... a time for planting and a time for pulling up .... He has a right time for everything." We realize that all we can do is to be happy and try to do the best we can while we are still alive. Of course, we are not suggesting "that whatever will be, will be" and we have no control over it. It does mean, that through careful awareness, we can discern the absence of the appropriate time for something such as the growth of a plant. In the final analysis, we might say there is a time for planting, ... a time for cultivating, and a time for pulling up.

Let's return to the discarded rose bush and the time for cultivating. More than likely with a whole lot of tender loving care, that rose bush would have survived. As I reflect on another gardening effort of mine, I was successful with reviving a plant. A small gardenia bush was on its last leg [so to speak] ... yellow leaves ... few leaves ... dead branches ... green leaves here and there. With the appropriate soil conditioner and regular watering, lo and behold, today I have a lovely, large bush with beautiful, aromatic gardenias.

Maybe what this is all about is focusing on the value of every single human life. No one is beyond the grasp of "saving grace." When all seems beyond the pale, let hope prevail ... give time it's due ... invest your best. God has shown us this in Jesus Christ. "While we were yet sinners Christ died for us." Moreover, "He came not into the world to condemn the world, but to save the world." It took a great investment, as one might say, capital, to claim humankind from disaster. It took the cross. So "work like everything depends on you; pray like everything depends on God."

Giving Your Best

JUNE 2, 2010

Memorial Day is a <u>United States federal holiday</u> observed on the last Monday of May (May 31 in 2010). Formerly known as Decoration Day, it commemorates U.S. men and women who died while in the military service. We could call this day "Sacrifice Day". On this day, we take time to remember the many women and men who gave their lives so others can live in freedom and security. I am reminded of a story about a soldier who gave his life in the fray of battle for his friend. A story is told of a soldier waking up in his hospital bed. The first words out of his mouth were, "where is Johnny?" Johnny was his best friend. They fought side by side. This soldier had been shot and was lying unconscious in an open field. Johnny crawled out onto the field to rescue his friend. He dragged his friend back, but while doing this, he was shot and killed. The soldier upon hearing this, cried. Johnny was his best friend and, with no hesitation, he put his own life in danger to rescue him. This is not an isolated story; but retold in similar settings over and over.

The battlefield provides for us scenes where people have given their lives without question to secure life for others. It's not just the battlefield, but again and again in everyday happenings, we find people having no concern for their own life and rush into a dangerous situation to save someone else. Possibly, the reason we lift such happenings up with such appreciation is this is more often the exception rather than the rule. The human proclivity is more toward self-preservation rather than self-denial. Thank God for that noble soul who forgets herself so that another might gain life in the face of disaster.

This is another reason why I believe in Jesus. "He did not count equality with God a thing to be grasped, but became a servant even to the death of the cross." The Apostle Paul quotes these words after he has suggested to the Christians at Philippi that they should think of others before themselves. This notion builds on the words of Jesus to the rich young ruler, "Deny yourself, take up your cross [as you care for others] and follow me. You can gain the whole world and lose your soul." Much of the discord in the world today is due to our predisposition toward self. The beauty about Jesus' teachings is his call to sacrifice not just for ourselves, but even for our enemy; those people who exercise little or no regard for our well-being. Maybe we all need to ask ourselves the question, "Really, how much am I willing to sacrifice for the well-being of others, for the development of a just society, for building a healthy community?"

Getting Away

JULY 28, 2010

My wife and I got in our car several weeks ago and motored across Tennessee to western North Carolina. We spent a week with friends we had not seen in over a quarter of a century. Some 600 plus miles east of Memphis at a higher altitude, we found a marked change in climate -- a welcome change. My wife commented when we returned home, "I had a good time." Good company and good weather brought a good time.

Last week, I wrote an article about how we are busy at work keeping the wheels of society going and our own lives afloat. The focus of the article was God's intervention in our lives to help us clarify what we are about and to give us the opportunity to change. The Christian message is "to believe in the Lord Jesus Christ and be saved from the destructive conditions in our life." We are more likely to see with each new day God's renewing presence when we accept that we are not perfect, but are pressing on to that high calling in Christ Jesus. Often, a change of pace, a different location and good friends give us the opportunity to claim a fresh perspective.

It is essential to "take time to be holy, speak oft with your God."

One of the commandments God gave Moses on Mt. Sinai was "Six days labor and do all your work, but the seventh day is the day of the Lord; in it, you should do no work." Let's move beyond a literal interpretation of these words to the core meaning. The story of creation in the Bible reminds us that after God created the world in six days, the seventh day he rested. The word rested does not mean he took a nap. It means he took a respite from the work of creation and meditated on what he had accomplished; he then said "It is good!"

Even our worship can become so commonplace that we fail to hear the Word of God expressed in a fresh and new way that brings newness to our life. Worship is the time when we are supposed to stop intentionally, the routine activities of our life to see and hear. Beyond the obvious with the eyes of faith we can see God's holy movement. Beyond the obvious with the ears of faith we can hear his guiding voice.

Back to the trip my wife and I took. Breaking the routine and taking a trip as we did is like that seventh day of rest. We are able to see and hear the spiritual realities of life without the interference of the clutter and clatter of the day-in and day-out happenings and interruptions.

Staying the Same

AUGUST 11, 2010

"We would like for things to stay as they are." Have you ever made this statement or been a member of a group that had this mindset? If you haven't, you want to be thankful. If you have, I would like to challenge you with the thought that this is a stultifying statement.

Life is always evolving and changing; this is the essence of growth and new life. To stay the same is to become planted in time and space. A little boy heard his father say the words, "I would like for things

104

to stay as they are." The little boy responded in his youthful wisdom, "If everything stayed the same, I would never grow up and enjoy the challenges of life as you have. You would never have grandchildren to love and pamper." The father, with a bewildered response said to his son, "I'm sorry son. In my interest to make life easy for myself, I forgot what I was denying you and what would be lost." I have tried in this brief discussion to explore what we are saying with the words, "I would like for things to stay as they are." Even if we wanted to do so and claim the fullness of life we couldn't do so.

Why are we so prone to resist change and want to put our feet in our present comfort zones? It seems obvious to me! Keeping things as they are requires little energy and less effort. We might say that it requires no investment of ourselves or our resources. It involves placing our security in the things of this world. Jesus said, "You can gain the whole world and lose your soul."

I imagine that many of the people reading this article are Christians. Let me suggest that there is a pronounced difference between having a Christian religion and a Christian faith. Religion takes shape by placing concrete forms of worship, ways of thinking and actions of living. We then commit ourselves to these as if they were our comfort blanket and we won't let go. The Christian faith is defined as the "assurance of things hoped for and the evidence of things not seen." By faith, we live with the assurance of an unfolding future filled with hope. In religion we live hanging onto the forms and ideas and ways in which we have become comfortable. Jesus calls us out of our settled ways to follow him and participate in the breaking of the new day that is always on the horizon.

Claim the Sunrise

SEPTEMBER 15, 2010

I officiated at the funeral of a member of my extended family.

The underlying theme of the meditation was "walking out of the sunset of today into the sunrise of tomorrow." I am reminded of the words of a hymn, "Day Is Dying in the West" ~ "When forever from our sight pass the stars, the day, the night, Lord of angels, on our eyes Let eternal morning rise, and shadows end." The movement of time brings the inevitable ending of a day with the beginning a new day.

It is not hard to see the funeral like unto the passing of time. At the end of each day, we find ourselves bring to closure all that we have been about, prepare for the night of rest in anticipation of the new day. We walk out of the sunset of today into the sunrise of tomorrow. For those of us who believe in Jesus Christ, the funeral gives anticipation to the new life -- as one might say, "eternal in the heavens." Jesus says to us that we should not be dismayed what'er betide. He gives us peace, an inner peace, which sustains us in the endings and beginnings of life. He speaks of a home not made with hands, eternal in the heavens. The funeral service enables us to celebrate the sunset of life in the death of our loved one. We know that tomorrow there will be the sunrise of a new life.

We took time during the funeral service to remember and say life was good. I am reminded that when God created the world, after six days, on the seventh, he took time to remember what He had done and said, "It is good." But that day of restful reflection becomes the springboard, so to speak, to claim tomorrow with a "fresh and living hope." We are able with assurance to walk into the sunrise of another day.

I know someone who has a routine through which she goes at the end of the day. She puts her pajamas on, washes the makeup off, brushes her teeth, spreads out the bedcovers. She then reads a bit of scripture, says her prayer, turns off the light and goes to sleep with the assurance that all is well. She wakes up each morning ready to live a new day, as she might say, "This is the day the Lord has made. Let me rejoice and be glad in it." When we reach any moment in time, whether it is the end of the day or the end of a life, by the grace of God we can "walk out of the sunset of today into the sunrise of tomorrow," knowing all is well.

Thanksgiving by Sharing

NOVEMBER 24, 2010

As this edition reaches your homes, you are enjoying your Thanksgiving meal. This is a time when family and friends gather around the table to eat well in appreciation for the past year. This national holiday is based on the time when the first settlers in this country spent time in thanksgiving for a good harvest with the anticipation of a harsh winter. They believed that God had blessed them and would continue to bless them on into the uncertain tomorrows.

A hymn that we often sing during this season comes to mind. The words ring out in my mind: "Now thank we our God with hearts and hands and voices." While Thanksgiving is a secular holiday, established by our government, it is based on a profound religious conviction. This notion is that "in God, we live and move and have our being." Jesus taught his followers a prayer which has come to be known as "The Lord's Prayer." In this prayer, we find the words "give us this day our daily bread."

I am reminded of the story of a preacher who said to the farmer, "I imagine you are thankful to God for the good crops this year." The farmer responded, "Well preacher, you should have seen my field when God was in charge and before I took care of it." Fortunately, most of us are not so arrogant to believe that God's providential care does not have a vital role in our continuing prosperity from day to day.

Thanksgiving is not merely a time to remember how much we have been blessed. It is also a time when we share our resources with others. An activity that is repeated year after year in our communities is preparing care baskets for others; this is one way we count our blessings, naming them to show what God has done. The story of Scrooge told over and over again at Christmas time shapes a beneficial change that is appropriate to note. Scrooge was transformed from a person who merely counted his money to a person who shared his money.

I often use the expression "conduits of God's love." We love because God first loved us. We can be a conduit of God's love by letting our thanksgiving for our many blessings reach out in loving care for others. Could it be that the best way to realize a blessing is to share our blessings with others? Yes, let us thank God this year, as always, with hearts and voices and sharing hands.

Living in Faith

DECEMBER 1, 2010

The Advent Season began last Sunday. This is the time we focus our attention not only on the birth of Jesus Christ, but on new beginnings. The birth of Jesus was God's announcement of a new beginning for the world. The good news of Jesus Christ is that God has destroyed the power of both death and sin over human life. I have a friend who has a terminal illness where death is imminent. This morning, I read words of encouragement sent to him that appeared on his blog. I thought I might share some of these words with you with the hope that these words will give you strength for the living of these days.

"Do not fear, for I am with you, do not be afraid, for I am your God. I will strengthen you. I will help you. I will uphold you with my victorious right hand." Isaiah 41:10

"Have you not known? Have you not heard? The Lord is the everlasting God, the Creator of the ends of the earth. He does not faint or grow weary. His understanding is unsearchable. He gives power to the faint and strength the powerless. Even youths will faint and be weary. The young will fall exhausted. But those who wait for the Lord shall renew their strength ... they shall mount up with wings like eagles ... they shall run and not be weary ... they shall walk and not faint." Isaiah 40: 27-31

"But we have this treasure in clay jars, so that it may be made clear that this extraordinary power belongs to God and does not come from us. We are afflicted in every way but not crushed; perplexed, but not driven to despair; persecuted, but not forsaken; struck down, but not destroyed." 2 Corinthians 4: 7-10

"We do not lose heart. Even though our outer nature is wasting away, our inner nature is being renewed day by day. For this slight, momentary affliction is preparing us for an eternal weight of glory beyond all measure, because we look not at what can be seen but at what cannot be seen; for what can be seen is temporary, but what cannot be seen is eternal." 2 Corinthians 4: 16-18

"What has come into being in Him was life, and life was the light of all people. The light shines in the darkness and the darkness did not overcome it." John 1:4-5

What If!

DECEMBER 29, 2010

The conversation was engaging. Two people were discussing the possibility of an event. One seemed to think "this happening was possible." The response from the other was, "What if nothing happens!" Then a third person sitting on the sidelines spoke out, "But, what if something happens!"

The world between something and nothing sometimes is likened unto the distance between the ends of the universe. The twain will never meet. Many of the conversations between people today, especially in politics and religion are shaped by, "What if nothing happens!" "What if something happens!" The tragedy of today's dialogues is that nothing is happening.

When we are honest with ourselves, we come to the understanding that neither the liberal nor the conservative today brings much to the table of useful living. The liberal should bring the challenge to be open to new ideas. The conservative should bring a call to responsible management of resources. But both are bringing their inflexible principles. To these principles, they attach themselves and their personal survival.

Too many people today are acting like two bulls fighting it out to the death. Yes, they are fighting for the control of it all. Whoever wins will eventually find themselves in another fight, and yet another fight. The end will be death to someone; the tragedy of this unending struggle for power could be the demise of the whole fabric of culture as we know it.

Times a Changing

MARCH 30, 2011

On the first day of spring, I turned another year on my calendar, in other words, I had another birthday. I am approaching that time in life of which the scriptures state, "Our days…, our lives are over in a breath – our life lasts for seventy years, eighty with good breath." [Psalm 90, sel.] Over the years. I have received many cards, phone calls and personalized greetings for my birthday. This was the first year that "birthday wishes" on Facebook came in such numbers that we would say "times are a changing."

The fascinating note is that I received birthday greetings from not only those of my own generation, but nephews and nieces, and younger friends near and far. The various social tools on the internet [such as Facebook and Twitter] have brought people in touch with each other for better or worse; in my case, it has been for the better. We are able to communicate with the passing of a moment where not too long ago it was the passing of hours, days and weeks. And the exciting note is that we can immediately respond. With a few words and the touch of a key, I have been able to say, "Thanks for the birthday greeting."

Just think about the communication journey we have been on this last century: letter, telegraphs, telephones, the internet with email, Facebook, Twitter, and the iPhone with texting. My wife and I have cell phones where we can talk to others. My grandchildren and my children have smart phones where they can text. My wife and I decided we want to communicate with our grandchildren in their way; we have cell phones that can be used to text.

Both the tools and methods of communication have changed [and will continue to]. I guess what this says is that those of us who have a foot at the portals of eternity [hopefully] want actively to engage in the remaining days of our earthly life, need to be willing to do a little changing. Otherwise, we may need to be satisfied with sitting in a comfortable rocker watching the moving stars and letting the rest of the world go by. What a dull life!

Laughter

MAY 18, 2011

I watch "The Virginian" on the western series on television. In a recent rendition, a Jewish tailor was talking to a young man who was bemoaning a personal problem. The tailor responded with the words, "Learn how to laugh." One of the words of advice I have given young couples during marriage counseling over the years is, "You need to have a sense of humor about life and about yourself. You need to learn how to laugh at yourself."

I have used an illustration from my New Orleans roots from time to time. In South Louisiana, crawfish are eaten with much delight. To the outsider, this is far from a delight; if enjoyed, it has to be cultivated. To the insider who has learned to remove the morsel of meat, the eating is approached with insatiable pleasure. This pleasurable undertaking would be lost without the addition of the appropriate spices. Let me suggest that a life without a sense of humor is like crawfish without flavoring. It would be bland and lost in routine.

There is a song that comes to mind as we pursue this notion of humor: "When You're Smiling, the Whole World Smiles With You." The words for this song continue with *"When you're laughing, when you're laughing, The Sun comes shining through. But when you're crying, you bring on the rain. So stop that sighing, be happy again. When you're smiling, keep on smiling ... The whole world smiles with you."*

There are a lot of happenings in life that could easily drape this earth with a black cloth of hopelessness and sadness. We well know that the more negative we are, the more negative we behave, and the more hopeless life becomes. Recently, in our country, and particularly across the South, tornadoes swept with much devastation and death. One college student who was in the path of the storm, and who had lost friends, said, "You just have to hold up your chin, smile and move on." A bowed head and despondent spirit cause us to become frozen in place. Whereas, a good laugh will give us the energy and determination to press on and claim a new day.

Don't Give Up

MAY 25, 2011

I have thoroughly enjoyed watching the Memphis Grizzlies during the NBA playoffs. The team is in the playoffs for the first time in a number of years. They were the last of the teams to qualify in their bracket; they then beat the top team to move on to the next level. They were in a dogfight to qualify for the finals in their division. Very few people, if any expected them to get this far.

They believed in themselves! They thought they could get this far and hopefully further. Several lessons have come to my mind as I have watched this team. The first of course is that they believed in themselves. It is fascinating to observe that a person [or a team like the Grizzlies] can have the ability, if yet they don't think they can accomplish an undertaking, then their chances will be appreciably diminished. Self-confidence is an essential ingredient for success in life. It brings together all of the positive energy in us. In contrast, if we don't believe in ourselves, this absence of belief creates uncertainty and the absence of that second effort. Let me suggest that self-confidence makes us possibility thinkers. And when we are possibility thinkers the next level of attainment is in our sights.

Another lesson I learned from watching the Grizzlies is the importance of teamwork. There are many teams in professional basketball that have several players around which the team is built. You take these players off the team and they are not nearly as good. The Grizzlies, in my mind, function more as a team. The players on the bench are as necessary for winning the game as the starters. The coach uses the strengths of the individual players when the game may require a different dynamic. In other words, one lineup and one lineup only, does not fit every game. Life has to be seen in the same way. There is not one answer to every problem. There is not one way to manage every task. Flexibility and versatility are key ingredients for the successful living of these days.

The third lesson is the importance of never giving up. This team plays the game until the final horn is blown. There are games where they were so far behind they couldn't catch up; but not many. In most of the games, their determination kept them as participators; and their persistence often helped them overcome. Life can be seen in the same way. In our journey through life, there are times when we get behind. Do we give up and throw in the towel? Sometimes we surely want to. I hear the Apostle Paul saying about his own life: "I have not arrived, I press on." The Apostle pressed on to claim the full gift of life in Christ Jesus; to realize the power of his resurrection and the fellowship of his suffering.

Man's Best Friend

MARCH 4, 2008

I have been reflecting on my life's journey over the last ten years since I retired. Such reflecting takes me up a number of rabbit trails. A rabbit trail is ~ it is a little trip off of the main road. Well, one of the rabbit trails I have taken is thinking about the pets in my life.

Let me first tell about a boxer we had when I was an early teenager. We live in New Orleans with a small back yard and houses very close to each other. Today, we would call such houses zero lot line houses. Back then such a category was unknown. Unfortunately, I don't remember his name … let's just call him Boxer. Back to my thought, Boxer was a very active dog. Let me share one incident with you. Boxer would start at one side of the small yard and when a cat would run through the yard, he would follow the cat over the fence -- actually clear the fence. Determined to control him, my Dad extended the height of the fence with very sturdy piece of wire. Well, this attempt to slow Boxer down became ineffective. He would grab the wire and pull himself over the top of the wire and continue his pursuit.

Actually, our Boxer and the German Shepherd dog we got when our two children were very young had much in common. Both were determined dogs and were not going to let what we did stand in their way of doing what they wanted to do. Does this sound familiar?

Sounds sort of like humans: if we've got any desire to accomplish something in life we are not going to let the barriers other people put up stand in our way. And we are not going to let other people super-impose their plans for us on our lives. It can be a good quality in life, as long as we are not destructive toward others in accomplishing our goal.

Gypsy, our German Shepherd, demonstrated a certain amount of self-determination. Gypsy was a female and pregnant with puppies. I thought that it might be good to build a nice dog house and area for Gypsy. I considered this to be a good project for me and my son, who was still very much a preschooler. The space we created was a perfect place for Gypsy to have her puppies; this is what I thought. There was an open space so she could move in and out at will.

The day came when Gypsy had her puppies. She did not bring them into the world in the newly built doghouse in that nicely creat-ed shady space my son and I build for her. She had her puppies under the next door neighbor's house. She had dug out a space where she could settle in and bring her puppies into the world in that relatively cool place. Well let me tell you the rest of the story.

My son and I crawled under the house and drug Gypsy's puppies from there to the place we had planned for her. It took very little time for Gypsy to drag her puppies back to the spot she had cho-sen. Determination to DO IT MY WAY was evident in both Boxer and Gypsy. Give your pets some recognition and respect for having a mind of their own. Also let's give those around us some credit and respect for having a mind of their own where we don't attempt to impose our will on them. Give others a chance to blossom in their own self-determination.

Careful Attention

JULY 9, 2008

One of my current projects is in placing Palisades Zoysia across my back yard. This is an attempt by my wife and me to create our Garden of Eden. We have been shaping what we consider a place of beauty. The yard is bedecked with a variety of flowers, camellias, gardenias, azaleas, and the list goes on. I usually prepared the beds. Becky designs the arrangements of flowers and does the planting. She is in charge of the watering. I cut the grass. I spray the plants and shrubs and apply the fertilizer. Together, we attack the weeds with determination. Whether or not the distribution of labor is equitable is not for debate. We enjoy together bringing beauty to God's creation and encouragement to each other.

Hopefully, you might be thinking at this point, "Thanks for sharing with the public this piece of your daily life." But also, you may be wondering where I am headed. As I set out the pieces of Zoysia this morning and then watered, I began to think that it sure takes a lot of attention to make this landscape of beauty. When we fail to water, the grass dries up and the tender flowers wilt. To maintain the yard with the anticipation of growth and the picture of beauty, we have to give it much attention.

These reflections on our efforts in gardening depicts a universal notion about every aspect of life. I think about my children's extraordinary investment of time and energy in their children, our grandchildren. And I remember how much time and energy went into the rearing of our children. We recognize that our families are part of a worldwide mural of people from every race and creed and nation. This mural portrays the natural human instincts to invest our lives in the health and learning and beauty of our offspring. Wonderfully so, such care is a valued expression of who we are, an expression of our love.

We might envision a companion mural. This mural would show the cities and towns, the mountains and streams as the domain of women and men investing themselves in bringing harmony to our lives together and preserving the creation in which God has made us the caretakers.

The challenge of these musings and visual murals is to realize what it takes to be about shaping and reshaping life, individually and together, so that each succeeding generation will enjoy a life of value and beauty. On these hot summer days, with the sweat pouring down my brow, I often ask, "why am I doing this." When I look out at the final results, I know why! This same question might be asked about our investment in our families, the larger community and the created order, particularly when there is pain and disappointment. Hopefully, we know why and would not do otherwise!

He Went Somewhere

NOVEMBER 12, 2008

Within the last month, I participated in a funeral for a new friend, Carney. He came to the church one Sunday several months ago; this was his first visit. He immediately expressed an interest in participating in the church. He has lived in Oakland about three years, though is a native to this area. Each month, a group of members gathers to consider plans for the congregation. The afternoon of his first visit to worship we had a meeting of this group. He was invited and came. He brought enthusiasm and a vision of a growing church. I believe that God sent Carney to our church to be a voice of encouragement.

Carney had visited a number of churches in the area and found this church to be the place he would serve his Lord. This visit to our church was not a chance happening. I believe that God moves in marvelous ways, his wonders to perform. God sends us people and opens doors of opportunity and takes happenings [both sad and good] to bring about his plan for our lives. God does not only do this for individuals, but he does this for groups of people, such as our church. While with us briefly, the time he was with us helped give shape to our future.

Carney died of an aneurism. He was just past 50 years in age. Several years ago, he had an accident on a four-wheeler and received a life-threatening injury. As an outdoorsman, he loved this world God has created, but the accident limited him and dampened his enthusiasm.

A neighbor mentioned to me just after his death that Carney seemed to be his old self. Well, I had not known Carney when he was his "old self." His new self did have enthusiasm for the Lord. But the week before his death, Carney and his wife and in-laws took a trip to Yellowstone National Park. This hunter and fisherman, a lover of nature, was renewed as he ventured out of himself into this expanded world touched by God's majestic hand.

Several weeks ago, I wrote an article about the importance of reaching out into other places and with other people. Carney did this with his trip to Yellowstone. He was set free to engage life with renewed interest and enthusiasm. Go somewhere, near or far, and you will find renewal for the living of these days. Believe it and do it and you will like it!

A Moment in Time

DECEMBER 9, 2009

I believe that the secret to the "good life" is not found in what is happening all around us, but what is happening inside of us. Both the good and the bad around us are but moments in time. Allowing ourselves to be captured by any one moment [good or bad] in time will keep us off balance. The weather, for example, changes where we never get what we fully want. Last Sunday, the weather was dismal. The attendance at worship was correspondingly dismal. I would have been shocked if the attendance had been like Easter Sunday; human nature does not work quite that way.

How do we live from day to day without getting caught up in the grist mill of despair and hopelessness? Such a disposition toward life can be a profound part of our daily routine when the clouds are dark and there is nothing significant looming over the horizon. The firm conviction that something good will happen while floating on the abysmal sea will keep hope alive and our eyes open for something good.

The overarching focus this time of the year is Christmas, the birth of the Christ child. In the Christian tradition we have just entered the Advent Season which culminates with Christmas. When we begin with Advent, not merely celebrating Christmas, we are reminded that God made a promise to the people of Israel that he would save them from oppression with the gift of a Savior. So we are gripped with the celebration of new beginnings. This new beginning empowers us with hope.

There were times in the life of the Hebrew people of when their circumstance created dark clouds over their existence. The history of these people might be described as the ebb and flow of good times and bad times -- particularly when they were told that they were to be blessed by their God. Then again, not-so-good times became extended occasions of hopelessness. They needed something that would empower them to live with hope, regardless of the circumstances around them. While God would send prophets to confront the people regarding their unrighteous ways, God would also send prophets to jack them up and infuse them with hope by extending them the promise of a better day.

Shaking the foundations of the earth by nature and disrupting the ordering of life by the interplay of nations became dismantling for the people. This has been and will continue to be ongoing phenomena for humankind.

Sure, such happenings can dismantle us and throw us into the snake pit of disaster … or as Jesus suggests in our scriptures, these can be the signs that the reign of God is at hand and we can rejoice "that nothing can separate us from the love of God" It is important to keep hope alive!

Easter, So What!

APRIL 7, 2010

Sometimes, I think Easter should be celebrated in the depth of the winter months. You might be thinking "What an absurd thought!" Easter in spring is a natural. The flowering trees with the green leaves and green grass are popping out all around us. This natural manifestation reminds us of the new life of the resurrection. The death of winter gives forth with the new life of spring. "Up from the grave Jesus arose like a might conqueror o'er his foes." What could provide more evidence of this new life we realize in Jesus Christ than the outcroppings of spring! What could be more reassuring than the warmth and growth of spring breaking forth out of the dark clouds and end of winter! The manifestation of spring is an excellent way of framing the hope of the resurrection.

The conditions on the death hill where Jesus hung on a cross were like unto winter … dark clouds, a barren hill and a sorrowful happening. For this reason, I think it would be better if we celebrated Easter in the dead of winter, rather than the beginning of spring. We would realize, in a more profound way, the overwhelming meaning of the resurrection event.

The natural order was not only dark and foreboding, but the social order was dark and foreboding. The demonic and death in all fullness had claimed the soul of humanity. The full corruption of life had reached its zenith. God in human form had reached out in unconditional love to recover a lost humanity. The full and utter corruption of the social order was displayed in the form of denial and rejection. The governing establishment crucified Jesus. The religious order that had nurtured him out of a sense of threat rejected him. The people in fear of their own survival hid from him when he was no longer of use to them.

The resurrection of Jesus is not merely an affirmation of a new life in the by and by. It is the realization that God has not forsaken his creation in spite of our tendency to destroy what is good and beautiful. It is the recognition of a new day not only in the cycle of nature, but by the action of a gracious and merciful God. Why not celebrate Easter in the depth of winter; it was in the depth of human degradation where humanity rejected God that Jesus was raised from the dead. "Up from the grave Jesus arose like a mighty conqueror o'er his foes."

Nothing Stays the Same

JUNE 9, 2010

When you are approaching eighty years of age, there is a tendency to think you know it all. As one might say, "I did a heap of learning over the last ten years." When Becky and I retired, we bought a new home. There were two lovely Bradford pear trees in the front yard; nothing in the back yard. We have gone to considerable lengths to plant additional trees and create flower beds to bring beauty to the landscape. Our thought was that the tress would grow and with proper pruning and fertilizing, they would add an elegant dimension to the group around our house. We have bought flowers and shrubs, planted, fertilized, and watered with the anticipation of healthy growth and beautiful flowers.

But we failed to include in the equation the wind and ice. Over the years, the two Bradford pear trees have been blown down with rain and wind. In early years, we planted two pine trees, a maple and two yeshiva cherry trees. The wind has toppled the two Bradford pears in the front yard, taken limbs of maple and pine trees. An ice storm broke a limb on one of the yeshiva trees. We have replaced the trees in the front yard with another Bradford pear and two magnolia trees. The trees standing were not so badly damaged that we have not been able with proper pruning to bring shape to them. But there is no guarantee that another stormy day or a heavy layer of ice is not part of the future, and more limbs will break or even trees uproot.

You might be thinking, "What are you driving at?" Namely, that nothing stays the same. Even when you do your best to keep things in the proper shape and order, there are unexpected happenings that can change the sheer landscape of your life. I have been fortunate not to have a tornado or a hurricane devastate my property; these storms are the full expression of the outside elements unsettling our lives. Death, accidents, the economy, and diseases are some of the happenings of life that alter, change or redirect the way we are caused to shape our journey.

When the first Bradford pear tree was blown down, we removed the debris and planted another tree. Sure, we didn't have to put up another tree. Life would have continued. But maybe putting up another tree represented beginning again. I believe that it is vital to take advantage of shaping new life in the face of a loss or tragedy. Built into the very essence of life is the thought that a seed must fall into the ground and die before new growth will come forth.

Advent Keeps Hope Alive

DECEMBER 8, 2010

We are in the Advent Season which lifts up the promise of a new beginning. New beginnings convey the beauty and rhythm of life and are as fresh as the morning dew. They are a form of re-creation. This is a time of change with the passing of the old and the coming of the new. But the time of this new beginning is not known. The Christian believes that God provides this new beginning in Jesus Christ. These are not easy times living in the shadow of tomorrow with uncertainty. Even with a promise.

What do we do? How do we plan? One might say that we keep hope alive. Hope is like a night light in a dark house. All of the lights are turned off. We have to be careful of the fear of stumbling over a piece of furniture or some object on the floor as we move about in the darkness. The only light available is a night light in one room of the house. We are not able to see clearly. The night light gives us a sense of space. Hope is like the night light; we are able to maintain some sense of the bright tomorrow with its fresh starts.

From time to time, we are caught in the tangled web of living. Very uncomfortable and uncertain, our cry might be, "what's the use" or it could be, "I believe, help my unbelief." Maybe, we celebrate the Advent Season with all of its implications because we need some reassurance that all is well when we find ourselves in the grasp of the uncertain. Imagine what life would be like if we allowed the tidal waves to shape our thinking or the conflicts to govern our behavior, or even the limitations of resources to control our ways. In other words, if we allowed those things that unravel life to govern us. We would either give in merely to existence or drive off the cliff in our fun mobile.

"How do I live each day?" is the important question to ask. True, God is working his purposes out as years succeed to years. He has promised us that the old is passing with the new before us. True, by faith in Jesus Christ we can realize this new beginning. We have a home not made with hands eternal in the heavens. But today is here with all of its uncertainties. I guess I am OK in my little world of reasonable security. But when I dwell on the uncertainties, I'm not sure! Where does my assurance come from?

Our assurance is also rooted in the way we live, believe it or not! Paul in his letter to the Romans gives us some clue. He writes about how to live with the awareness of a fulfilling future; namely, the coming of the Lord and a new age. These are his words: "Set aside works of darkness and put on the armor of light. In other words, live honorably [lives free of wastefulness, recklessness, quarreling, jealousy]." Faith in Jesus Christ gives shape to honorable living. We can keep hope alive by the way we live. "Every day, every day keep the little light of hope aglow."

Yes, "Morning has broken, like the first morning. Mine is the sunlight. Mine is the morning. Born of the one light Eden saw play. Praise with elation. Praise every morning. God's re-creation of the new day."

What the Difference a Day Makes

MAY 4, 2011

"What the difference a day makes!" It was not one day. It occurred on the third day after his crucifixion that the tomb of Jesus was found to be empty. With eyes of faith, the Apostle John could easily have said "Up from the grave he arose like a mighty conqueror o'er his foes!" The Apostle Paul poignantly wrote that "if Christ be not raised from the dead, our faith is in vain."

Easter is more than a celebration of the resurrection of Jesus and the believer's assurance of eternal life. It's the realization that all of creation has been set free from the grip of death. We can live in terms of life; not the black hole of nothingness. The Apostle Paul also wrote, "O death where is thy sting; O grave where is thy victory? Thanks be to God who gives us the victory in Christ.

I believe that when we speak of all creation being set free from the grip of death, it means more than eternal life for those who believe in Christ. It means that we no longer live in terms of death. What do you mean, Sam? Just think about how much of your life is determined by the imposing presence of death. We do so many things as we prepare for death and so many things to fight off the inevitability of death. Just think about how much the overarching cloud of death determines what you say and do. It grips us with fear and a strong sense of nothingness. It pushes us as we try to avoid it by living in the realm of self-glorification.

Once we are set free from the fear of death, we are able to live with a robust joy and a personal sense of strength. We no longer live for ourselves, trying to create eternity out of time. We try to create eternity out of time by putting ourselves in the forefront and protecting ourselves at any cost. When death no longer has its control over our lives, we are able to deny ourselves and claim life as we strive to do justice and live in love.

It is not the life beyond this life about which I am concerned. By God's grace, we are saved. It is this life with all of its threats and potential fears that overwhelms us. To be free of the control of such threats and no longer afraid of nothingness is living on the hallelujah trail. Yes, yes, "thanks are to God who gives us this victory in Christ."

3. Affirm Others/ Realize Self

The key that unlocks the door to a hopeful life is in the title of this chapter, "Affirm Others/Realize Self." The emphasis is to put others before self, or at least give the other person an equal place at the table of life's expectations. Often, in everyday life, we realize that human proclivity, at best, affirms others when it is advantageous to self-realization. A term I learned during the Civil Rights Movement of the last century fits well here. This term is "enlightened self-interest." This means "I will help another when it is advantageous to my own interests." In these articles, I take this a step further; I am recommending that we begin with the affirmation of others apart from any concern for self. This notion of placing others before oneself admittedly stretches the fabric of our existence.

This sense of care for the other person(s) is essential to living in community. The realization of community is indispensable for life, liberty and the pursuit of happiness for all, and ultimately for one's self. Affirming each other's value is paramount. The progression of thought moves us to recognize the importance of even loving our enemy.

How vital it is to affirm the value of those who differ from us! We then are able to pursue our rights in a healthy context of mutual care. Where conflict occurs, we pursue our interests, recognizing the value of others; this means that we relate to others assertively (with care for them) rather than aggressively (with disregard for them). We acknowledge that people with whom we differ have something worthwhile to contribute. We do not see them as merely an obstacle to our success, but as people who have the same interests for the fullness of living.

No person is an island; we all live on the same big island. The issue is whether we choose to live together, seeking the well-being of everyone or as individuals merely looking out for our own well-being. Choosing to live in our separate spaces diminishes the sense of community and, in turn, the possibility of our own fulfillment. Therefore, enlightened self-interest becomes a primary pursuit of the other person's interest.

Will this island become a battleground of self-preservation or a place of self-realization? I have become more aware that my personal fulfillment occurs when I choose to no longer pursue a life of self-serving, but one of self-giving, and even at times self-denial. This is not easily done; self-denial realized in self-giving seems to be contrary to our human nature.

Living is like a team sport. Take basketball, for example. A strong competitive team is achieved, day in and day out, as each player accepts responsibility for the game plan and develops respect for each other. In the social arena, it is necessary to recognize that all people have at the core of their existence a striving to live and to achieve personal fulfillment. The fiber that holds us together is a sense of respect and mutual care for each other.

The articles in this chapter show many ways to affirm others along with denying ourselves. There should be the assumption that those with whom we differ may have something worthwhile to contribute. It is necessary to remain sensitive to others, even if we believe we are right. How vital it is to be courteous and respectful to others, even if we disagree with them! This leads to the need to set aside our self-preoccupation. We are then able to be open to the other person's ideas and sensitive to their needs. This means getting out of ourselves and getting into the mindset of another to see with their perspective.

When we take these steps toward one another, we are acknowledging a willingness to learn from others. The outcome of all this is the awareness and realization of our own personhood. We not only gain a sense of personal value as we turn away from ourselves toward others, but we also grace them by affirming their value. The world becomes a better place to live.

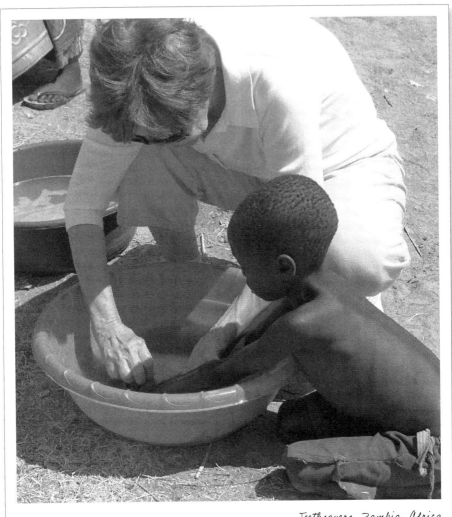

Teethsavers, Zambia, Africa

I am *recommending* that we *begin* with the
affirmation of *others* apart from our concern for *self*. SBL

The Laine Garden Mosaic

"Such hope can be realized when we are willing to recognize our identity as we take up our cross of abiding care for others." SBL

Love your Enemy

FEBRUARY 22, 2008

At every level of human life, people are in conflict with each other. We find conflict in the home, in the community, between nations and even within churches. Where there is conflict people are engaged in adversarial relations. As we walk anew with the "Lord in the light of his way, what a glory he sheds on our life." Of the many ways and words of Jesus we might muse over, his words "Love your enemy" are overwhelmingly crucial in today's world. These words of Jesus are timeless. These words of Jesus have profound implications for living these days at the beginning of the 21st Century. If we are going to live and enjoy this world of trees and streams, of birds and animals, of towns and cities God has created then we have to love not only our family and friends, but also our enemies. Our Lord has "got the whole world in his hands", and his firm and gentle command is for us to love "it all."

I've always felt that Jesus is not only my savior from sin and death but a special person in the span of humanity. He gives me guidance for relational living at every level of the social order. The reason I believe Jesus is special is because he breaks through the limitations of narrow love where we love only family and friends. He leads us to the fresh and verdant fields of loving those who love us to loving those who even dislike us and want to do harm to us.

I've introduced two words that might need a bit of fresh explaining: love and enemy. Love as a verb is an expressed care and regard for another person. We might describe our enemy as the person who hates us and wants to do us harm. Jesus said that "it is easy to love your family and friends, everybody does that; the difficult thing is to love your enemy. I say to you love your enemy, those who hate you and want to do you harm." [paraphrase].

132

The gripping realization is that our enemies are as close to us as across the dinner table and as far from us as across the waters in Afghanistan. The irony is that near or far -- our enemy sees us as a threat to their existence and a thing [not a person] that should be destroyed. So if we are going to build caring families and helpful communities and cooperating nations, Jesus' command to "love your enemy" is profoundly relevant.

Finally, let me say it is necessary to you. <u>WHEN</u> we deal with our enemy merely as a threat, we are controlled by anger, envy, jealousy, sorrow, regret, greed, arrogance, self-pity, guilt, resentment, inferiority, lies, false pride, superiority, and ego. <u>WHEN</u> we show care and regard for our enemy, we become a conduit of God's love {joy, peace, love, hope, serenity, humility, kindness, benevolence, empathy, sympathy, generosity, truth, compassion, and faith.} Far better to have the fresh winds {love} of a new day shape our lives, than the harsh winds {hate} of a stormy day tear our lives apart!

A Kind Heart or a Mean Spirit

MARCH 11, 2008

What will it be: a mean spirit or a kind heart? Should I kick him in the head or gently touch him? You might wonder where these words are headed! Two words when contrasted describe two ways of relating that are as different as night and day. One comes out of the darkness of a life preoccupied with oneself; the other comes out of the light of a life predisposed toward the well-being of others. These words are aggressive and assertive.

Every day, we find ourselves engaged in relationships with a variety of people. The approach we take will have much to do with the outcome. I guess we're ready to tackle these words: aggression and assertive.

When I act aggressively I am primarily, if not all together, concerned for myself. I am reminded of the thought, "I had a party and invited me, myself and I to the party." No one else is important. Everything I do is for me, myself and I. I don't view or think about the other person(s) as being valuable. So in any encounter where I find myself acting aggressively, the other person(s) would exist for my benefit. I am not at all concerned about what happens to the individual, only to the extent of realizing my own personal gain. My behavior may be manifest in a strong and destructive reaction or a very quiet devious reaction. Either way, the person with whom I am engaged is just a "thing" to be used or abused.

When I act in an assertive way, I truly care for the person. I may not agree with the person; actually, I may strongly disagree. But I am not going to do anything that might cause harm to the person. As I am engaged in conversations about my life and my future, my position is not so important that I will do just anything to get my way. Hopefully, I will always remember that this person is an individual much like me and I will certainly try not to bring harm. Actually, I will try to bring encouragement.

I believe that when we act aggressively we not only bring harm to the other person, but also bring harm to ourselves. I am reminded of Jesus' words, "You can gain the whole world and lose your soul." I may gain much by running roughshod over others, but in the final analysis, I lose a bit of myself in the transaction. When I act assertively [and show care for others] I show the qualities of grace and mercy in myself and draw out the qualities of mutual care and respect in others. I may not win every transaction, but I will surely enrich and enhance every life. What will I be: aggressive or assertive?

What Shall it Be?

APRIL 2, 2008

What shall it be? Self-serving! Self-giving!

The word, sin, is has a significant place in the language of the Christian faith. Explore the implications of this word and we might realize a number of expressions: breaking the law, not doing God's will, killing, stealing, hating, missing the mark, and the list goes on and on. I would like for you to explore with me the idea of self-serving as a way to describe sin, the destructive way of life. Let's use the expression of self-giving as the healthy way to enhance life.

I am reminded of a saying, "I had a party and invited me, myself and I." Would you not call this the height of self-serving? In our extended local area and across the country, the discussion of politics is in the air. As politicians flaunt their wares, I have come to see how profoundly the human animal does so much to serve self and often, in the name of "doing for others." One of the many characteristics of wisdom is not perfection, but the ability to take a serious look at oneself, then ask the following question about all of our actions and relationships: *Am I strongly interested in the well-being of others, or am I just simply trying to serve myself?* When we can effectively ask this question and honestly answer it, we are moving in the right direction.

There are a number of tests we can use to measure our self-serving ways. Let me suggest just one at this time. How do you handle criticism of your ideas and actions? Do you try to learn from the criticism or do you react defensively? I have come to realize that we often make our ideas, for example, an extension of ourselves. We tie up our ego in what we think. It's like our hand at the end of our arm; our ideas become an attachment to who we are. When our ideas are challenged, and we react, we show that we feel attacked. Since I don't believe I am perfect, I have come to realize that my ideas are not absolute.

When we can deny idealizing ourselves and begin to "live for others," we are able to become what I call a conduit through which God's love passes. It's like fresh water flowing through a still pond. The clean water brings fresh oxygen to the still pond. When we are open to letting God's love flow through us as love and justice for others, we are renewed and refreshed. It takes cleaning up the self-serving system to become a self-giving conduit.

Caught up in Self

APRIL 23, 2008

I called my brother this last week to check on him. My sister had shared with me that he had fallen. When he answered the phone, my opening words were, "Bub, I understand from June that you fell and hurt yourself." It did not take long for him to share with me the details of his fall. What I wanted to do was remind him that I had just had a birthday, which he had failed to recognize. I thought surely he would have called me on my 75th birthday.

Life is ironic! My thoughts are on my brother being caught up in himself; yet here I go calling him, hoping he will recognize my birthday. It is astonishing how much we humans operate in terms of our own personal interests and correspondingly, neglect showing real care for others.

I am reminded of the words of Jesus on judgment. Jesus said, "Judge not that you be not judged for the judgment with which you judge, you are being judged." Another way of saying this is, "When you are critical or judgmental of others, watch out because you may be saying something true about yourself." Watch out that you are not pointing your finger at yourself. While I was finding fault with my brother's lack of interest in me, I was pointing a finger at myself.

The Apostle Paul in one of his letters encourages people to "consider others better than yourself. Have the mind of Christ, who did not count equality with God a thing to be grasped but humbled himself, taking on the form of a servant." Paul following in the footsteps of Jesus made a 180 degree change in his life. He changed from wanting to do everything for himself, even his service to God. He became like Jesus whose guiding way in life was to deny himself and become God's loving presence for others. He gave up his life that others might have life -- life abundant.

Giving up our life for others is so contrary to the way most of us do things. The irony of life is that the greatest, most genuine joy comes when we deny ourselves so that other people can share in the blessings of a fuller life. Think about this notion! It's true, isn't it! Try to be kind to someone today, with no thought of yourself. Try it, you'll like it!

I Feel your Pain

MAY 6, 2008

"I feel your pain" is a way of saying: "I understand what you are going through." Jesus was standing before a large group of people with his disciples in front of the crowd. He spoke the words which we traditionally call "The Sermon on the Mount". We find a series of statements about happiness. He said, "Happy are the merciful, for they shall receive mercy."

I remember nearly half a century ago when I was in seminary and a visiting professor shared the meaning of the statement: "Happy are the merciful ..." Dr. Barth rephrased these words, "Happy are those who can get in the skin of another, understand what is going on in their life and respond with empathy" We are inclined to think of being happy when we get something. The suggestion here is that happiness comes when we are engaged in understanding another person. Another word used for happiness is blessed. The thought is that when we "really" understand another person we receive a blessing.

The Apostle Paul wrote "Don't do anything from selfish ambition or from a cheap desire to boast, but be humble toward one another. Always consider others better than yourself." One way of effectively doing this is by focusing attention on the other person and trying to understand where they are coming from. In order to do this, we have to get out of ourselves and stop thinking about what is only important for us.

Most of the conflict in life happens because the opposing sides are thinking mainly about themselves. They are out to protect their own self interests. It is when one or both parties are able to start thinking about the difficulties, the needs, the interests of others that the conflict can be resolved and new opportunities for life begin to happen.

Jesus tried to drive this point home over and over again. He would say, "Deny yourself. You can gain the whole world and lose your soul." When you find yourself in conflict with someone, then take a step back, put your interests aside and try to put yourself in the other person's shoes. Ask yourself questions. What are they thinking? Why are they upset? How do they see what is happening? What are they thinking about my response? You will begin getting out of yourself and hopefully empowering yourself to reach out to them. They will thank you for your consideration. And in turn, you will be blessed.

A Helping Hand

MAY 13, 2008

When I initially began this article, the people of Suffolk, Va. had just suffered a devastating loss from a tornado. Many injuries and buildings were destroyed. "The destruction looks like a war zone." The television pictured the mayor sharing a report on the efforts by many to restore community to the area. These efforts remind us of familiar scenes that occur over and over again when devastation comes.

Since then, other areas of the Mid-South have been devastated by tornados. Now, this week, the people of South Asia have lost thousands and thousands of people with a cyclone sweeping across the land. The overwhelming suffering of people and the destruction of property by the hand of nature doesn't seem to stop.

We are reminded of the essence of human nature. On the one hand, we live in our separate spaces and pursue our personal agendas. On the other hand, we come together to reclaim our communities near at hand, and those far away, especially when we are faced with a disaster. Deep within the heart of people is a sense of empathy for others, not just family and friends -- even strangers and enemies. Time and time again, we have seen people respond to others caught in disastrous situations.

Jesus told a compelling parable about a Samaritan who helped a person who had been beaten along the road. The religious leaders, too busy with their church duties, passed by the man. The Samaritan, a second class citizen to the Jews, took time and placed the person in a place where he could recover. Jesus told this story when the strong emphasis of help was for the neighbor, not the enemy. The outcome of the story was that everyone should be treated as a neighbor. I think Jesus was saying that we should not let our religious perspective, our social position, even our busy life get in the way of doing the Godly thing; namely, showing care for others.

With eyes wide open, we should come to the realization that we do not have to be a Christian or even a religious person to show care. Although a Christian surely is one who expresses care not only for "my kind" but for all people of the world, even our enemies. We talk about the importance of natural resources, especially oil and natural gas, for survival. The most valuable resource for healing and health and wholeness in the world is our ability to express unconditional care, a common human resource that is abundantly available.

Perfection

MAY 20, 2008

A picture hanging crooked. A piece of silverware in the wrong place on the table. The failure to obtain all As on the report card. The list goes on and on. It even becomes more critical regarding its impact on daily living. A child is born with a birth defect. Each one of these, and many other expressions of seeming imperfections, have an impact on the way we live our lives. Our responses to these circumstances says much about ourselves.

Our responses to these so called imperfections can drive those around us to the wall or encourage us to do the best we can. We can bemoan our situation or try to find ways to improve our surroundings and the lives of others involved. One might say that perfections are in the eye of the beholders. Several weeks ago, I shared a story about a child who had a brain tumor which miraculously disappeared, but left the child less than what she might have become in the measure of human beauty and intelligence. However, she grew up to be a loving young adult.

I think that we are caught up in a society that strives for the perfect … the perfect in academics, sports, physical beauty. We find ourselves elevating and acknowledging those who attain the highest level of achievement. We look with diminished appreciation on the so called "lesser" persons of society. I am interested in how the news media has described a particular group of the voting population, as the less educated. No doubt, it is important for a variety of reasons that a person get the very best education possible, but our value or worth as a human being is not measured by our education or our material resources or spiritual piety. I am reminded of the words of scripture: "While we were yet sinners Christ died for us."

Let me invite you to hear the words of Jesus when talking about perfection with Jewish leaders. He [Jesus] said to them [paraphrased]: "The laws say to love your neighbor; well I say to you love your enemy. It is easy to love your neighbor, those who love you. It is something else to love your enemy, those who hate you, despise you. Be perfect as your heavenly Father is perfect." Elsewhere, Jesus said to turn the other cheek when someone has wronged you. The essence of perfection is not measured by our talents or accomplishments, but by who we are inside.

This is graduation season. We should want the very best for our children and our children should seek to achieve the best as they reach out to claim their place in the world. But let us remember that to be perfect as God is perfect equates not to the excellence of achievement but to the ability to embrace with care both friend and foe in the daily engagements of life.

Finding Common Ground

JUNE 10, 2008

One of the most significant realizations in life is that each person sees life in their own unique way. Why is this realization so significant? It is significant because it moves us outside of ourselves and causes us to recognize in the words of William Shakespeare, "all of the world is a stage and all the men and women merely players." I am not the center of the world where everything revolves around me and emanates from me. This realization allows me to be open to another person's thoughts and ideas as being of value. More importantly, it empowers us to accept people with whom we interact as persons of value. When we do this, we move beyond mere conversation to real communication -- beyond living alone, to living with others in positive expectation.

How do we buy into this important world of interpersonal appreciation? We have to realize that each person has a system of thought. This system comes into being as a result of our own DNA, our social and cultural environment, and our religious and personal development. I have mine! You have yours! I look at life from my perspective! You look at life from your perspective! I remember the title of a teaching film that often comes to mind, "The Eye of the Beholder." This film invites us to recognize that each person brings something special to the conversations about life. When we acknowledge this, we will travel a long way up the road of effectively dealing with others.

In order for a person to progress toward opening doors and creating new opportunities for building strong relationships, the person needs to learn how to communicate, not just have a conversation. This was something Jesus did so very well. People, especially religious leaders, would approach him with their dogmatic positions. He would challenge them to think deeply about what they were saying or asking. He didn't argue with them. He listened to them and helped them reflect on what they were saying. Even though he did not agree with them, by listening he was treating them as people of value. He did not back down, but he did not attempt to overpower. He did not see them as enemies or adversaries but potential friends.

We will come to understand that living with others requires finding common ground, that place from which we can think together. We begin by accepting other persons as valuable and listening with appreciation. The outcome hopefully will be not my way or your way, but a common way [a way that brings fresh air, clear skies and a calm sea].

Affirmation

JULY 23, 2008

Several weeks ago, a close friend of mine died. He was my senior by about 20 years; this would mean he lived to the ripe old age of 96. He played basketball and coached at Texas Tech University in Lubbock, Texas for over 17 years. He possessed the combined qualities of sound self-esteem and humility, rarely found together. This friend had an effective way of affirming people in their endeavors. I was asked to write a word or two to be read at his funeral. Since I was not able to attend, I would like to share with you some of my words:

Over the seventeen years I served as Pastor of Westminster, Polk affirmed and supported me in every way. From the very beginning of my ministry at Westminster, he reached out to me. This young 36 year old at the time, appreciated his support as I undertook the leadership of this strong and vibrant congregation. This support and appreciation for my ministry continued throughout. He and Stephanie [wife] threw garlands of acknowledgment my way out of the sincerity of their hearts. You know, we ministers, while we realize God loves us, we always need an occasional word of love and appreciation from persons in the pew. I'm not sure that I was as wonderful as Polk and Stephanie affirmed, but my love and thanks go out to them for their encouragement and love. Being the son of a minister, he knew, he really knew!

My purpose in sharing these words is not to bring attention to myself, but to stress the importance of affirming others. His affirmation throughout the years became an aid in my personal and spiritual growth. Over the years, I have not given this part of my life much thought. The opportunity to reflect on our relationship has brought out this latent insight. Polk's and Stephanie's encouragement and love reinforced the basic assurance I felt about myself. God places people in our paths along the way ... people who enable us to "keep on, keeping on."

Let me express a brief word on God's behalf. I am reminded of the words we often hear from the pulpit, namely, "While we were yet sinners, Christ died for us." That was [and is] God's big way of affirming us.

I want to use this unique experience to recognize the importance of affirming people: our children and spouse, family and friends, and even the strangers along the way. Self-worth is a significant piece of the human psyche. Affirmation helps to build self-worth. When we feel valued, it is easier to get up in the morning and be about the business of living with purpose. When we feel valued, it is easier to enable others rather than criticize them. When we feel valued, it is easier to deny ourselves and bring joy to others. I've often heard that it is better not to say anything about another, if you can't say something good. Just imagine what a better world we would have if we all moved about affirming other people rather than finding fault with them. The rest of the story comes in the form of a question ~ Have you affirmed someone lately?

What Needs Changing?

AUGUST 6, 2008

Several weeks ago, I wrote my article on "Change." I posed two questions that we needed to ask when dealing with change. The first: what is changing and how do I go about dealing with such change? The second: what is it that we need to change and why? I went on to suggest that "change is inevitable."

When I finish an article, I go to the spell check on the computer to see if I have any misspelled words. A misspelled word will appear with a red underline. The spell check gives several choices, two of which are ignore or correct. I can ignore the correct spelling or correct the misspelled word. This is rather the way we approach the issue of change. We can ignore change or make the necessary corrections to deal with what is changing. We can change what needs to be changed or leave things as they are or life as it is and suffer the unfortunate consequences.

In reflecting on this matter of change, I have formulated a basic principle to apply the question, what needs to be changed? This basic principle is, *"Deal with the whole and not just the parts."* This notion can be translated into other expressions. "Consider everybody and not just yourself." "Prioritize, but don't forget the goal." "Focus on the person and not the individual." "Help shape a community that values all people." Finally, I am reminded of the Apostle Paul's advice when he built on Jesus words, "Love one another as I have loved you." Paul writes, "Count others better than yourself; have the mind of Christ, he did not count equality with God a thing to be grasped, but humbled himself." Change should always be made for the well being of everyone and the created world of which we are an essential part, not just for one self.

One of the greatest needs to empower good and affect change is to choose leaders whom we might call <u>servant leaders</u>. These are people who see themselves simply as servants of the people, rather than benefactors for themselves. These are people who are making decisions for the well-being of all the people, not solely for themselves and their political party or religious group or even their own community. We are a nation of the people, by the people and for the people. Yes, and we the people need to move out of our narrow world of self-interest into a world where we "deal with the whole and not just the parts" ... with a concern for "all the people" and not just some of the people. <u>What needs changing?</u> <u>Leaders that are in "it" only for themselves and lack a real sense of concern for others</u>. Give of your best, so others might realize their best.

Someone to Know

SEPTEMBER 17, 2008

Last week, I wrote an article entitled, "Someone to know ... Something to do ... A place to go." The article grew out of the observation of an aging family member whose world had collapsed into a small space of existence. I began to reflect on what it is that we humans need to sustain a life of meaning. The outcome of my reflections was the above title. I did not have the space in last week's article to elaborate on each aspect, so I thought I might spend time over three weeks exploring the meaning of each. This week, I want to reflect on what it means to have "someone to know."

When I shared these thoughts with my wife, she immediately suggested that the object of "know" should be someone to love. We all need someone to love. But I intentionally chose the word, know. I then proceeded to share with her why the word, know and not love. I am not referring to knowing about someone, rather actually knowing someone -- and being known by someone. Such a knowing means experiencing their presence and understanding their inner self. It means being aware of their purpose for living and feelings toward life. You are able to hear their thoughts without their speaking a word. You are able to understand their approach to happenings without explaining.

Of course, such empathy with another person happens when this knowing is mutual. One might call such a relationship a genuine friendship. I have often heard people say that a genuine friendship is hard to come by and difficult to sustain. I remember when I was a child learning the song, "Friends, friends, friends, I have some friends I love ... I love my friends, and they love me ... I help my friends and they help me ...."

The point I was trying to make in the previous article was that it is helpful for a person, whose world is diminishing in scope and accessibility, to have a friend in the full sense of the word. No doubt it is upstanding when spouses have such a relationship. Are you not touched when a person speaks of his or her spouse in the terms, "She or he is my friend." But I believe that we all need a person whom we can call, "my friend" outside of our family associations.

It is compelling that Jesus thought of his disciples as his friends; he would say that they were more than his disciples, they were his friends. And we find in the Gospel of John where Jesus said that a real friend is willing to lay down his life for his friend. We are aware of the fact that Jesus made the ultimate sacrifice of being crucified for his friends. I guess this is what friendship truly means, namely, the willingness to forget yourself and invest your life in the well being of another. It means touching hearts, and not merely touching hands. Being such a friend is hard, particularly when the other person is unable to give as much in return. Be thankful that God enables you to be a friend to others.

This is the Day the Lord has Made

OCTOBER 9, 2008

A friend of mine sent me the following poem, entitled, "Today." *"I may never see tomorrow; there are no written guarantees ... And things that happened yesterday belong to history ... I cannot predict the future ... I cannot change the past ... I have just the present moments ... I must treat it as my last.*

I must use this moment wisely for it soon will pass away, ... And be lost forever, as part of yesterday ... I must exercise compassion, help the fallen to their feet, ... Be a friend unto the friendless, make an empty life complete.

The unkind things I do today may never be undone, … And friendships that I fail to win may nevermore be won … I may not have another chance, on bended knees to pray, … And I thank God with a humble heart for giving me this day."

This poem reminds me how valuable is each day of life. It also brings to remembrance my own life journey. On the first day of my retirement, a little over 10 years ago, I collapsed and came close to death. Then three years later after climbing the Acropolis in Athens, Greece upon my return home and a visit to the doctor, I was immediately admitted to the hospital for bypass surgery. I believe that God has and continues to give me life. This gift of life is not just for my own pleasure. It has been given me to live each day … to "live each moment wisely" where I am able to enrich the lives of others.

Several years ago, I saw the movie, "Pay It Forward." This is the story about a young lad who, along with his classmates, was challenged to write a paper by his teacher. The theme of the paper was how he could make the world a better place. The idea of his paper was to choose three people for whom you can do something selfless. When you do the selfless thing, tell them to pay it forward. When they ask what you mean, tell them to choose three people … do a good deed for each and say to them "pay it forward."

In the final analysis, we are talking about what is the core value of human existence. Is it to "eat, drink and be merry for tomorrow we may die"? Or is it to make the world a better place for others. It doesn't have to be either. It can be both. I would not suggest that the many activities, from our hobbies to our outings to our excursions, are not of value in giving meaning to our life. But the core value that keeps our life together, alive and fresh and forward-moving, is living for others and thankfully affirming God as our life-giver.

We might want to take a lesson from the young lad in "Pay It Forward," at least try to do one good deed for someone each day. My wife and I were returning home from a short vacation. I was stopped and behind me was a long line of cars. To my right, there was a driver trying to get out onto the street. I let him move in front of me, and said to my wife, "I've done my good deed for today." It is not this deed I particularly lift up, but the thought that a "helping hand each day" can enrich another's life, yes, and make the world a better place in which to live. We love because God first loved us. Pass it on! Pass it on!

Going Somewhere

OCTOBER 29, 2008

As you read this article, I will be returning from a two-week trip to China, Thailand, and Cambodia. I've been asked, "Why in the world are you going to those places?" My first response was, "Because I have the opportunity." Since I retired from fulltime ministry over 10 years ago, my wife and I have had the privilege of traveling many places inside and outside of the United States. We began our journey abroad with a trip to Scotland and England. As the years added to years, we found ourselves in the eastern Mediterranean climbing the Acropolis, and then riding on the back of a camel in front of the pyramids in Egypt. Then there was central Europe at Christmastime visiting the 12th century cathedrals. Rome and Florence and Venice brought the romance of Italy to our closest touch. Those far away places of the United States ~ Hawaii and Alaska ~ also shaped our awe of God's creation. But I can't miss out our trip to Africa where we stayed in luxurious hotels in South Africa and slept on the ground in the bush country of Zambia. When I return from this present trip, I will have embraced just one more part of the world.

What is the value of all of this? I am not sharing this with you just to say, "Gee, look where I have been!" These were not just trips we took. These were adventures into the lives and cultures of other people. I am not the same person I was 10 years ago before my wife and I embarked on these various trips. Some people will say when they come back from such trips that they appreciate the United States even more. I do not go abroad to enhance my appreciation for this great nation; such, I don't need. I visit these different places and peoples with the notion of learning about life from other people and cultures.

What I have learned first and foremost is that when we do not reach out and touch others, both at home and abroad, our perspectives on life remain narrow and limited. When we are willing to leave home and travel to places, near and far, our lives are enhanced and our life is enriched. I am reminded of a hymn, "This is my Father's world and to my listening ears, all nature rings and round me sings the music of the spheres." The thought in this hymn is enhanced for me when I visit other places and people throughout the world.

I Love you and it's OK

DECEMBER 10, 2008

"Love is a many splendored thing." As we make our way toward Christmas, we focus our attention on a love that is truly a many splendored thing: God's love for all humanity expressed in the gift of his Son, Jesus Christ. I would like to talk about this love by telling a story.

A number of years ago, my daughter asked me to come and babysit for the grandchildren over a weekend. My wife was not able to help at the time. On the afternoon of the second day, the children and I had a point of difference earlier. As the day came to a close, I sat with them and tried to engage them in a conversation. My eight year old grandson responded, "It's OK Grandaddy!" At the same time, my three year old granddaughter folded her arms and puffed up. Later, when I took her up to bed, she asked me to tell her a story and sing a song. Before leaving the room, she touched my arm and said, "Granddaddy I love you, it's OK."

I've been giving a lot of thought lately to what God's love means. You see, of all the ways love is described, when we speak of God's love for us, we use the word agape. Agape love is unconditional love. In other words, there are no strings attached. There is none of the notion that "I will love you, if you love me back" or "I will love you if you do what I want you to do." There is none of this with God's loves for us. There is more of "I love you and it's OK."

There are a couple of other ways we can reference love. I will love you because you are beautiful and attractive to me. Yes, you turn me on. Or there is friendship love. We would say, "I love you because you mean a lot to me ... we have a lot in common ... I enjoy being with you. We just have a good time together and I can depend on you." I believe in the final analysis both of these loves usually place expectations on the person we love. We expect them to enhance our romantic notions. We expect them to be our friend, that trustworthy companion. Both of these loves are part of the human package [still important]; but neither one captures the essence of unconditional love which is abiding.

Unconditional love brings the gift of life to us; and says "I love you and it's OK" with no expectation. God loves us this way! We can love each other this way by the grace of God. This love is truly a many splendored thing.

See the Value

DECEMBER 17, 2008

How easy it is to think negatively about life! How often have you found fault with what others are doing! How often have you denigrated the efforts of others in the community? I've noticed that we humans have a tendency to be critical of the activities and undertakings of others. I have recently questioned a project in the community where I live. One of the weekly newspapers this week had an article on how this project would benefit the community. A thought crossed my mind. Maybe, if I asked myself the question ~ What are the ways that this project [or any undertaking of others] can be of value to the community? I might come to the realization that value can be found in what I might be criticizing.

The outcome of this brief dialogue about this project caused me to realize how crucial it is to consider the value of something before I reject it. When I was actively involved in ministry, I would make a suggestion when engaged in considering a new undertaking: "Make a list of the pros and cons of what was being considered." Even if this is done, the considered project might be rejected, but you would have given the project a fair hearing.

Have you ever asked yourself why you are so inclined to be negative toward the suggestions of others? Give this some thought! Some of the answers to this question shape up in terms of our own insecurities and personal arrogance. Maybe we believe no one else can do anything better than we can. We may see things in a restricted and limited way. Or we may have a valid position but fail to recognize there may be more than one way to accomplish something. The bottom line is we are often unable to see or think beyond the small world we have created.

For example, we in the United States have a tendency to draw a map with our country at the center of the world. This is unfortunate. My recent trip to China, Thailand, and Cambodia helped me reinforce a notion I have. This notion is "to have something worthwhile to contribute to life, people don't have to be like me or think like me." My way is not the only way! If you would like a great surge of freshness in your life, start living with this thought, "My way is not the only way. There may be another way!"

What a Difference the Cross Makes

MARCH 18, 2009

"In the Cross of Christ I glory towering o'er the wrecks of time." There is a song titled, "What a difference a day makes!" I want to put these words before you: "What a difference a cross makes." I have on my wall above a prayer bench a display of crosses. Many shapes and colors ... crucifixes and empty crosses ... all reminding me of that one cross ... among the three .... On Golgotha where an innocent man was being crucified as if he were a common criminal. We are told that this was a just human suffering and dying for the unjust.

There are certain happenings in history that have changed the human landscape. The most current happening was the planes flying into the twin towers on September 11. We know how dramatically this event changed our lives. Christ's death on the cross has changed life dramatically and could be said to be the focal point of history. We proclaim our personal salvation from sin and death because of our Lord's death. We also follow an entirely new paradigm of dealing with others because of our Lord's death.

We have not only come from "death to life," we have also come from dealing with others out of retribution to dealing with others out of unconditional love. I was reading in I Peter 3, *"Because Christ also suffered once for sins, the just for the unjust, to bring you to God, by being put to death in the flesh but by being made alive in the spirit. Finally, all of you be harmonious, sympathetic, affectionate, compassionate, and humble. Do not return evil for evil or insult for insult, but instead bless others because you were called to inherit a blessing."* The thought pops into my mind "what a difference the cross makes".

We are implored to recognize what happened on the cross. It was truly an act of the just for the unjust. Such an act ... such a notion ... was foreign even to the most generous minds of that day. Imbedded in the thinking of the world into which Jesus came was the notion that men had the right to retaliate … at least take equal retribution; yes, you take from me, then I have the right to take from you in equal fashion. The notion was expressed as an *"eye for an eye, and a tooth for a tooth."*

The cross of Jesus brought the world from the notion of "take in kind to be kind to the unkind." I think of Jesus' words [paraphrased] when he says *"love your enemies, even those who take awful advantage of you. Do not just love your neighbor; even the heathens love their neighbors. But love your enemies … love those who despise you and persecute you and say all manner of evil against you falsely, for great is your reward in heaven."* Not to mention, your sense of well-being on earth. What a difference the cross makes!

March Madness

APRIL 1, 2009

We are in March Madness. The conversations in some circles … the sports on TV -- are all about basketball, basketball, basketball. While athletics for some may be overplayed in our society, one thing we learn from sports, particularly basketball, is the importance of playing as a team. It's revealing how ineffective a team can be, even though they may have superstars, when the players do not play together as a team. It is inspiring how a group of players working as a team can be astoundingly successful.

There are four words that I want to share with you in my thoughts about the importance of participating in life as a member of a team, not merely as an individual. These words are duty, discipline, devotion, and denial. Using words starting with a "D," we should be able to remember.

First, there is duty. I do it because I am supposed to do it. I may not want to do it. I know that I should do it. It is a matter of what is right. It is a matter of my responsibility to the team, the group, the church; even to myself as a person of worth. We are good Boy Scouts. Remember the Scout motto: "Duty to God and country".

Let's take a look at discipline. Part of discipline is training ... getting prepared ... keeping our life under control. In actuality, life has at least two components to the "living of our days:" first, there is preparation and then there is action. Living out the things for which we have been preparing describes the action. If we're not prepared, we are going to fall flat on our face and we'll let the team down. The team may be our family, the church, the community or whatever group to which we belong.

The next word I want us to investigate is devotion. The words from a hymn come to mind: "Blessed be the tie that binds our hearts in Christian love, the fellowship of kindred minds is like to that above." Devotion is the tie that binds us to each other and to God. Surely, if nothing else drives us, duty needs to be there. We need to be motivated to live a disciplined life because we know it is the best thing to do for our own well-being. But the binding dynamic of our entire life is our devotion to our God and each other. Such devotion is expressed by a deep passion for what we are about and for the other members of the team.

The last word that comes into play is denial. The downside of failing to be dutiful ... of resisting discipline ... of being shallow in devotion is our <u>preoccupation with our self</u>. Our responses to the challenge might come in words, such as, "I am too tired", or it takes too much effort, or there is something else more valuable to me, or what brings me pleasure and satisfaction is more valuable than my commitment to what is right and faithful. The Apostle Paul in introducing Jesus' self-denial, writes "think of others before yourself."

Until we are able to forget ourselves, we will not be effective participants in life. When we get off the bench, put off our own ambitions, and participate with others in the game of life; how glorious life will be! Don't forget the four Ds for a full life: Duty, Discipline, Devotion and Denial. This is what enables a team to win! This is what enables us to find fulfillment in life!

What will it Be?

APRIL 15, 2009

Somewhere along my journey I was introduced to two words. These words are quite useful in describing the ways we deal with others. Hope you are asking the question, "What are these words, Sam?" Aggressive and assertive. The outcome of these two ways also is separated by miles. We are aggressive when we are thinking only about ourselves. We are assertive when we show genuine interest in the person(s) with whom we are engaged.

I want to say that "life is an activity of repeated negotiations." These negotiations occur in the home, place of business, school, church -- whenever and wherever we find ourselves to be interacting with people. Our goal in life should not be merely to get our way. Our life should be lived with the desire to accomplish our goals with a real concern for the well-being of others. Much of the damage to our economic framework today is due to the "greedy" who live by the rule "my way is the only way."

Jesus Christ presented a radically different way of life. He grew up in a world where the acceptable thing was to pay back in kind; in other words, to exact from others who have wronged you, at least equal retribution. The familiar phrase is "an eye for an eye; a tooth for a tooth." In his day, an enemy was an enemy; and should be treated as such. Jesus strongly encouraged people to love their enemy. Don't merely love your neighbor; love your enemy. Treat them as you would treat your family or your neighbor. Treat them as people of value and worth. Jesus went beyond the suggestion to meet them halfway. We find him saying "if someone slaps you, turn the other cheek". My Lord's goal in life was to restore relationships. This is what God has done in the life, death and resurrection of Jesus Christ. This approach requires a real investment in the well-being of others.

The Apostle Paul saw the light of the glory of God in Christ Jesus. He followed in his footsteps while expressing this same motif. He writes the Christians in Galatia, "We must not be proud or irritate one another or be jealous of one another. Help carry one another's burdens." In Philippians, we find these words: "Don't do anything from selfish ambition or a cheap desire to boast, but be humble toward one another, always considering others better than yourself."

The future of our relationships ... the future of our community ... the future of this world depends on the paradigm where people are willing to meet others more than half way. It may depend on our willingness to love unconditionally those with whom we disagree, even our enemies.

Revival!!!

MAY 6, 2009

This article provides the rest of the story or the flipside to last week's article on "Survival". I suggested that survival means "doing whatever we need to do, and no more, just to remain alive." Recently, I suggested several survival situations. A loved one dies; the person grieving continues to live in the initial stage of shock and does only what is needed to stay alive. From day to day, a woman is knocked around by an abusive husband and remains in the situation. A person has trouble getting around and spends all of his time in front of the TV. For these and many others who only survive, the value of each hour is lost, and the days pass over into the oblivion of tomorrow, rather than the sunrise of a new day.

Before I launch into what it means to break out of the "survival mode", I would like to visualize a picture of this mode. I am thinking of the person whose loved one has died, and he or she is only surviving. People are accustomed to saying about their loved one's death, "she or he has passed on." Surviving in such a situation might be seen in terms of our loved one having passed on [I prefer to use the word death] to a better life, while we are just hanging on. The phrase, hanging on, can be used to describe any condition of survival. The tragedy of just hanging on is that we are not breathing new life, rather stagnant air ... our life is a merry-go-round of seeing and doing the same thing over and over again. We have to find a way to let go rather than hang on! When we let go, we can break out.

One of the goals in life is to "live in the revival mode." William P. McKay wrote the lyrics to the hymn, "Revive Us Again." The last verse sounds the note, "Revive us again, fill each heart with thy love; May each soul be rekindled with fire from above." These words suggest two elements for revival, namely, love in the heart and fire in the gut.

This time following Easter reminds us that Jesus came into the world to give us life, the abundant life. He does this by setting us free from our deadness and preoccupation with ourselves. He makes us alive again. He does this by infusing love in our heart -- a love for those who are living without forsaking those who have died. He does this by giving us a renewed passion for living, namely fire in our gut. He gives us the freedom to break out of merely surviving and to claim the possibilities of a new tomorrow. The secret of a revived life is a renewed love for those around us and a deep passion to walk humbly with our God in the light of His ways. Such a walk empowers us to claim a new vision for the living of these days.

Mother's Day

MAY 13, 2009

This last weekend, we observed Mother's Day. Cards were given. Special family gatherings were held. Gifts were shared to express appreciation to our mothers. Churches made particular mention and spoke special prayers. This is a day when we say, "Mom we love you, we thank you, and we recognize you as the best."

Early "Mother's Day" was mostly marked by women's peace groups. A common early activity was the meeting of groups of mothers whose sons had fought or died on opposite sides of the American Civil War. In its present form, Mother's Day was established by Anna Marie Jarvis, following the death of her mother on May 9, 1905; she campaigned to establish Mother's Day as a U.S. national, and later an international, holiday. This expression of appreciation for our mothers is worldwide.

The note I want to strike regarding mothers is the sense of destiny they often have for their children. There are at least three mothers in the Bible who saw in their sons a divine calling. Of course, first and foremost is Jesus' mother, Mary. We read in the gospel of Luke the song of Mary where she expounded on the role of Jesus as the "hope bringer" to the down trodden of the world; the messenger of justice. Then there is Elizabeth, the mother of John the Baptist who was called the forerunner of Jesus. Both of these women cherished the role of carrying in their womb these men of holy destiny. In being chosen by God, they felt humbled to share in God's eternal plan. They embraced their sons with the full capacity of their nurturing love as they prepared them for adulthood.

Another woman of the Bible who is of special interest to me was Hannah, the mother of Samuel. Hannah had difficulty having a son. She prayed to God to bless her with a son; within her prayer, she promised to dedicate him to God. My parents blessed me with the name Samuel. My mother's father was named Samuel. It has not been revealed to me that they had the Samuel of the Bible in mind. After my mother's death, my father did tell me that she prayed upon my birth that I would be a minister. And I can remember from my earliest years my mother saying to me that "God has a purpose and plan for your life, Sam."

Both mothers and fathers have the potential of forming nurturing relationships with their children and of claiming a sense of destiny for them. I think women [yes, our mothers] innately bring nurturing to their relationships in a special way. Yet, I have seen fathers who have become the primary nurturers in their family. Over the years, as we are weaned from both of our parents, there continues to be that eternal bond between parents and children.

But today we want to give attention to our mothers. When Jesus was on the cross, he asked the disciple John who was standing by his mother at the foot of the cross to take care of her. Our mothers are truly special. Let us remember that God places our mothers in our embrace to care for them always as they have so wonderfully cared for us.

A Kind Action

JUNE 18, 2009

I shared with you an event at Wrigley Field when in Chicago. Today, I want to share another event from my visit to Chicago. While in town, instead of using our car, we took advantage of the rail and bus facilities. As I mentioned last week, we rode the rail to the ball game. I had a truly pleasant experience while riding the bus back to our hotel after spending a morning at the zoo.

By the end of the morning, after seeing birds and animals and reptiles with a brief pause for refreshments, we were ready to return to our hotel for a rest and a new adventure in the afternoon. I have a stick for hiking and walking excursions; it helps my balance when my pace is accelerated. I prefer the walking stick to a cane; I think of King David in the Old Testament when he was a young shepherd. I got on the bus with my walking stick.

The bus was crowded. Becky, my wife, was able to claim a seat. Austin, my grandson, and I had to stand. Here is where my story takes shape. There were two ladies sitting at the front of the bus. The front seats are along the windows facing the aisle. I was standing in front of the two ladies. I came to learn that they were mother and daughter. The mother was about my age, in her seventies. That would make the daughter, late forties or early fifties. She insisted on getting up and giving me the seat. I felt terribly embarrassed. Sure I was tired. Sure, the walking stick was helpful to me, but I did not see myself taking the seat of a lady. She insisted. I sat down. We were strangers and she gave me her seat. We carried on a delightful conversation as she held on and stood in front of me until they disembarked.

Why am I writing about this incident? Here was a person who could have kept her seat; she did not have to offer her place and insisted that I take it. Why? It all grows out of a sense of care and concern for others. She saw me as an older person and someone who needed a more stable relationship with the bus, rather than standing. She did not have to think about it. She responded spontaneously! Multiply this act of courtesy a thousand times, a hundred thousand times from city to city, from hamlet to hamlet and imagine how much better the world would be. It would be a better place. Courtesy and respect in whatever arena we find ourselves are the commodities of this better place.

The next time you have the opportunity to be courteous and respectful to another person, do so, and the world will be a better place. As we find in the words of a song ....." It only takes a spark to get a fire going, and soon all those around can warm up to its glowing. That's how it is with God's love once you've experienced it; you spread his love to everyone; you want to pass it on."

Sin ~ Learn About Me!

JULY 29, 2009

The word sin is heard from pulpits time to time. This is not just a word used in religious circles. It is a word that describes a fundamental malfunction of the human psyche. When I was a boy, a long time ago, I had to learn what we call in the Presbyterian Church, "The Catechism". This is a little book of questions and answers about God and God's ways. One of the questions is "What is sin?" The answer to this question is "Sin is any want of conformity unto or transgression of the law of God." Bluntly speaking, one way of defining sin is "not keeping the law. "When we don't keep the law we bring harm to others and ourselves.

In the church, we believe that the law is codified in the Ten Commandments. The first four have to do with our relationship with God. We are to place God first in our life. We are not supposed to use words that demean God. We are to worship God, particularly on a special day of the week.

The last six commandments have to do with the way we treat other people. The key word we might use to sum up these laws is respect … respect for people, their person and their property. We come to learn that honoring our parents is vital. The commitment people make in marriage, needs to be respected. Killing, stealing and desiring something that belongs to another is hurtful and destructive.

We often think of the Ten Commandments as laws telling how to behave and treat others. But the law embraces a larger perspective. When we live within the bounds of the law, society is healthy, and all people benefit. The law is for the purpose of creating a stable society where we feel safe and can realize our God-given potential "to be a little less than God with dominion over the creatures" [Psalm 8:1] Not God, but a little less than God.

Lawlessness has a way of infecting a society. Like any infection, it spreads and eventually cripples society. Well, we have let lawlessness get out of hand -- manifest in excessive street violence, greedy money grabbers and a growing prison population. Passion and greed, the poison of the law, are our waterloo.

How do we go about dealing with this extensive problem? Reinhold Niebuhr, a mid-twentieth century theologian, wrote "the reason for the law is the sinfulness of man." And yet, the reason for Christ's death is the recognized need for forgiveness. We need tough love. There are times when we don't keep the law and the restraints of society are necessary for the well-being of all people. Hence we need to enforce the law with the realization that man has a proclivity toward sin ... while recognizing the value of all people.

Sin ~ Learn Even More About Me

AUGUST 19, 2009

I hope that the articles on sin have raised some questions in your mind; such as, "*If everyone believed in God, does it mean sin would be eliminated?*" One of my retired friends spends much of his time sharing thoughts from here and there. Recently, he circulated these words: "Without GOD, our week would be Sinday, Mournday, Tearsday, Wasteday, Thirstday, Fightday & Shatterday." Here, he is describing a broken human existence without the reality of God in our life. In the full sense of the word, this is true. We have a deep need to find harmony in our lives; this happens when we find our existence in God. But the mere belief in God does not necessarily alter a week of Sinday, Mournday, Tearsday, Wasteday, Thirstday, and Fightday and Shatterday.

How do we break out of this no man's land of partial belief? I am reminded when one of the disciples saw Jesus after his resurrection. He had trouble believing even when he saw the nail marks on Jesus' body. His response was, "O Lord, I believe, help my unbelief?" We first have to admit that we see "through a glass darkly." Yet there is always the opportunity to see clearly. This clear seeing happens when we come to know God as he knows us. We continue with words from the scriptures: "Now abide faith, hope and love; but the greatest of these is love." (I Cor. 12:13)

When we focus our thoughts on love, there is so much we can say. In this context, I want to emphasize that love refers to a life shaped by relationships, our relationship with God and each other. A genuine belief in God is the result of a genuine relationship with God; awareness of this is important. There is a song that captures this notion entitled "Trust and Obey". I would like to share the first stanza of this song: "When we walk with the Lord in the light of his Word, what a glory he sheds on our way! While we do his good will, He abides with us still. And with all who will trust and obey."

Faith is not merely the worship of an Almighty God, but trust in an ever-present God. **<u>Sin is diminished with trust</u>**. This trust comes from a close relationship with God, a relationship of intimacy and appreciation. Jesus said that he came to fulfill the law and the prophets. Remember how he summed up the law: "Love God with your whole being and your neighbor as yourself". Where there is love there is God, for God is love. I have a piece on my key chain with four feet side by side on one side and the following words on the other: "My precious child, I love you and would never leave you. When you see only one set of footprints in the sand, it is then that I carried you."

A Tribute

SEPTEMBER 2, 2009

Last week, the nation celebrated the life of a powerful and effective U.S. Senator. Ted Kennedy died. I know that many of you who will be reading this article may have a negative attitude toward this man. He is a liberal and has a mark of disgrace from his younger years. If you feel this way, I encourage you to move beyond your mindset and think about his journey through many tragedies.

A review of the tragedies and other events in his life hopefully cause us see the way he dealt with life as a challenge to all of us. Three brothers died early in their life, one in a war and two by assassination. His nephew was killed in an unfortunate plane crash. Two of his children have had cancer, not to mention that his death came because of cancer. His first marriage crumbled. He was responsible for the death of a young lady because of his reckless ways. And yet, he rose above the many changes to be an advocate for the prosperity and health and well-being of others.

It is important sometimes for us to move beyond our focused and narrow thoughts about others to express thanksgiving for their life. Not only express thanksgiving, but also realize that we can learn from those with whom we disagree as well as, agree. So often, people allow the tragedies and difficulties in their life to extinguish the fire in them, the zest for living. They succumb to the despair that grips them. They lose the heart to live. We are told that the driving forces in Senator Kennedy's recovery from these "down times" in his life were his love for family, his faith in God and his genuine concern for others.

Words from a hymn come to mind: "Time like an ever rolling stream bears all its sons away. They fly forgotten as a dream dies at the opening day." Time bears us away particularly when we get caught in the tide of the destructive forces of life. The tide drags us under when we lose control, often because of fear. We are able to swim against the tide and fight the undertow when we are in control.

I believe we are in control of our life when the love of our family captures us, when our faith in God guides us, and when a concern for others drives us. In times of tragedy and difficulty, we may stumble for a time, but we will not fall. "Our help is in the name of the Lord who made heaven and earth. Let not your heart be troubled, let it not be afraid." "Rise up with wings of eagles; run and not be weary." Keep the faith! Always believe there is a future! Remember, the sun sets on our yesterdays and rises for our tomorrows.

Valuable

SEPTEMBER 9, 2009

I wrote an article on "The Journey" recently. The theme of the article dealt with how we come out from under the shadow of death along our earthly journey. The answer to the how was directed toward realizing that we are valued. But I never explored the notion of what it means to be valued.

This last week, I preached from the book of James in the Bible. James wrote to a people considered as being of little value in the eyes of the world. These were the early Christians. We find these words penned by James: "What God, the Father, considers being pure and genuine religion is to take care of orphans and widows in their suffering and to keep oneself from being corrupted by the world." As I read and reflected on these words, I said to myself, out loud, "Ah ha, this is what it means to be valued."

All around us, the sights and sounds say something quite differently. What is being said and heard is that to be valued in certain circles equates to prominence, wealth, prestige, and accomplishments;

the list goes on and on. In our society, the poor person, the meek person, the uneducated person [again the list goes on] describe the world from which we want to escape, and look upon as being of little value. We might conclude that the world says power, position, and prestige give value to life. And in our heart of hearts we know that this is not true. Possibly, true in a fleeting moment, but not in the eyes of eternity. Maybe this is the reason why James urged the people to "keep oneself from being corrupted by the world."

Let's look at the first part of the scripture reference. "Pure and genuine value [replacing the word religion] is to take care of orphans and widows in their suffering." These are the disregarded, the trampled and the helpless peoples of the world. They are without power or position or prestige. Why is it that my life is valuable because I show care for these people? The answer might be because it elevates me to the noblest expression of life; for in so doing, I am living by the will of God and expressing the image of God. The person that brings life and hope and joy to others gives value to their life. This has become a conduit of God's love. We get a sense of our own value as we bring value to others.

Stressed Out

SEPTEMBER 16, 2009

A song comes to mind, "When you are weary and cannot sleep, just count your blessings instead of sheep and you'll go to sleep counting your blessings." Wouldn't you say it is necessary to find some useful ways to deal with the times when you are tired and pushed to the wall? A good start is rest. But we can't always just stop those moments in life when conversation gets a little heated.

Do you have those moments in time when you are engaged in conversations, discussions, interactions [call it what you may] with others and frustration sets in? You don't seem to be getting your point across. The other person seems to be getting more aggressive or more defensive or more reactive. That person may be as cool as a cucumber and your temperature keeps rising. Then frustration sets in. You find yourself to be reactive. It has been said that when blood stops flowing to the brain, from which you can stay sane and sensible, and settles in the visceral area, where you operate on emotions is when you lose it. Your voice gets louder, and your words become harsher. You put on gloves to engage in combat.

The battle begins and the damage starts mounting up. You say things you don't mean. The outcome is phrased in such words as "Oh, I wish I had not said that!" (To yourself, more than out loud.)

The crucial thing is, "What could I have done to keep myself out of such a tail spin?" I want to ask you to explore with me the way to peace before the walls come tumbling down -- maintaining sanity before those insane moments happen.

Of course, if you can anticipate "those tenuous moments," then a proper rest or even withdrawal from the routine would be helpful. There are a few little things you can do; they might seem trivial, but they work. If you are in conversation with a family member or a close friend and the exchange gets intense, you might say "time out," signaling with your hands, as well as your words. Another thing that works is to just "bite your tongue." That will slow you down. Sometimes just clearing your throat or taking a deep breath will interrupt the intensity. I'm sure you can suggest other ways.

But in the final analysis, our inability to keep our cool happens because we are more involved in ourselves [what we believe, think and want] rather than a deeper concern for others or even the truth. Jesus repeatedly challenged the people around him "to think of others more than you do yourself." You might achieve in most situations a positive response if you follow Jesus' advice.

We May Be Right

SEPTEMBER 30, 2009

I ended last week's article with the words: "But in the final analysis our inability to keep our cool happens because we are more involved in ourselves, than in having a deep concern for others or even the truth." Jesus repeatedly challenged the people around him "to think of others more than you do yourself." You will realize one up on any situation if you do!

In your pursuit of your position or the truth as you see it, you may be right. My Lord, Jesus also pointed out to his disciple, "You may gain the whole world and lose your life." Let's rephrase this as "you may gain a point but lose the relationship." To be a winner and make the other person a loser does not make you a winner. As one has written "to make both persons winners should be the goal."

But you might be thinking "if I compromise my principles -- the truth as I see it --, then what do I gain?" If we would continue to use Jesus as the model of interpersonal relations, we would emphatically state that no one wins if we give up our principles for the sake of peace. Because, as Jesus said, "We would be building the relationship on sand rather than solid ground. The rain comes and washes the sand away; whereas, a house built on solid ground stands, remains." [paraphrase] So it is vital to establish our lives on the truth [as one might say, in terms of what is right and true and just] to achieve a good life with others.

I imagine that as you read this article you are wondering where I am going! The ultimate goal in life is to live together in mutual care and respect. We may accomplish much for ourselves by standing firmly on what we believe is true. Unless we pursue what we believe with a respect for others, the instruments of destruction can cause havoc and dismantle relationships. Maintaining relationships is essential to bringing genuine fulfillment to everyone.

The tragedy of life is that everybody does not operate in this way. The pursuit of self-interests is often stronger than a genuine care for others. Jesus emphasizes that the guiding principle for life is unconditional love, which is a willingness to deny oneself for the well-being of others. From time to time following this guiding principle may require personal loss. But let us not forget that thinking of others more than oneself is "the real way, the real truth and the real life". Try it, you will like it!

A New Friend

OCTOBER 14, 2009

I shared with you recently an overview of a trip my wife and I took to Egypt, Israel and Jordan. This week, I would like to introduce to you a new friend. We spent three days touring Egypt by way of a boat cruise of the Nile River. We began at Zokor and ended at the Aswan Dam. We stopped at other cities along the Nile. At each stop, we were introduced to the history of Egypt by way of the temples unearthed from the wind-driven sands of the past. Our guide, Hassan, brought to life times past as he described the ruins of these structures of antiquity.

Hassan is a young man in his thirties. He is married and has two sons. One delightful aspect of the trips I have taken is getting to know the persons who open the windows of insight into the places I visit. Hassan can claim Sudan as his ancestral home; this country is south of Egypt. He lives in Kom Ombo, one of the cities along the Nile where we stopped to view one of the ancient temples.

We got into a discussion about his life's story. This led to a discussion about education in Egypt. I asked him if he had gone to school to prepare to be a guide. He showed such an articulate understanding of Egypt, both ancient and current. In times past, public education was established through college for all the residents of Egypt. English is taught as a second language to all from elementary school. He said that this opportunity for education opened the doors for a career as a tour guide. Otherwise, he would have been a farmer. He was not saying that farming is of lesser value; rather, his education gave him an expanded opportunity.

I had the feeling that he had a genuine concern for me. We were not just a group with which he shared information. I was pleased that I was able to take the extended walks to the various sights. From time to time, there was uneven terrain where my steps became somewhat uncertain. He would say, "Put you hand on my shoulder, cousin."

He became for me a living person who was truly engaged in life. He had an enlightened awareness of the past and a clear understanding of the current world order. I realized a genuine connection with him because of our mutual concern where all nations would lay down their "swords and shields down by the riverside and study war no more."

Managing Relationships

NOVEMBER 11, 2009

This article began with the title, "Resolving Conflict" and ended up with "Managing Relationships." I think we more often try to manage a relationship to our benefit rather than resolve a conflict to the benefit of all parties. Possibly, one of the greatest needs in the world today is to learn how to get along. This is true at the individual level as well as the international level. But let's face it, it is not easy!

Instead of giving you a list of "what to do," let me try to shape the task. Could it be that what is needed is "getting out of our own skin and getting into the skin of the other party." Hopefully, said with some profundity, but to implement this notion is far from being easy.

This is the first move that both parties need to make even to get to the table of reaching peace and realizing prosperity. The process might be described as removing the barriers, opening the channels of communication and reaching a new dynamic of living. These descriptions could be laid out in terms of actions.

How do we go about removing the barriers? We perform this action by forgetting self and getting into the skin of the other person. Jesus often spoke of denying yourself to engage life effectively. The most significant aspect of "conflict barriers" is to look at life from merely our own perspective. The Apostle Paul writes that it is essential to think of others more than you do yourself. Getting self out of the way enables us to "get into the skin of the other person." This means understanding what the other person(s) is thinking and feeling. You may or may not agree, but at least hopefully are communicating.

When we are able to engage in this two-fold action, we then have begun to open the channels of communication. To open the channels fully, we have to demonstrate that we actually hear and understand our adversary. This means we have to listen. What are they actually saying? To know what they are saying, you have to hear beyond their words to their thoughts. And even beyond words and thoughts, to their feelings. Let them know that you understand them and are sensitive to them and then a breath of fresh air and a ray of sunshine begin to come forth.

We often talk about meeting people halfway. We have to do more than following the halfway rule. Take, for example, two people at the end of a bridge. In order to engage the person, sometimes you need to be ready to go more than halfway.

The last word is mutuality! One person, one group, one nation can't accomplish this alone. Both parties have to be willing to take these actions. Then and only then will peace come and prosperity be realized.

My Sisters' and Brothers' Keeper

FEBRUARY 3, 2010

I attended an honors ceremony this last week for middle school children. Across the width of the gym, children stood. Boys and girls, children of various national backgrounds, racial and religious groups were part of the gathering. Since it was a gathering of middle school children, they were of different sizes and shapes. Some were well developed and others meager in their physical structure; some were quite confident and others a bit unsure about themselves. As I looked at these children, my thoughts reached forward to ten, fifteen, twenty years from now. These will be the citizens of our communities. Our schools are not just educating children to do well for themselves, but giving shape to tomorrow's society.

This educational system which has become an integral part of our cultural fabric is the life blood of the future. What the children are taught today will strongly influence how the communities are built and how the world is engaged tomorrow. Our concern should be that we educate children to create a society where we are truly "one nation under God indivisible with liberty and justice for all." Because of understanding, education should be the BIG one, which is the foremost priority of the building blocks of our society.

The quality of education a person receives should never be determined by the economic level or the cultural status of a person or even the mental capacity. When I was in the pastorate, I conducted a vocational guidance program. This program was for the purpose of helping children understand their God-given gifts regardless of their social status or their jobs and emphasized their value. I was fortunate to grow up in New Orleans where rental homes on the side streets and very expensive homes on the boulevards brought children of diverse social and economic backgrounds into the same public schools. In a good public school system we all were enriched.

Nor should the role of education only be to prepare each individual to reach their highest potential. I believe that building a caring and just community needs to be part of every educational system. It is just as important to teach history, social studies, government, philosophy, religion and the arts as it is to teach mathematics and science. Unless we do all of this, we have a limited tool box to build the world God intends for his creation.

The everlasting chord that holds us together and builds a society where all people realize their inalienable rights of life, liberty and the pursuit of happiness is a deep and abiding sense of mutual care and respect for each other. I truly am my sisters' and brothers' keeper!

Getting to Know You

FEBRUARY 17, 2010

I am certain at some time, you have looked someone in the face or passed them on the street and said to yourself, "I would like to know this person!"

Oscar Hammerstein wrote these lyrics: *"Getting to know you, getting to know all about you. Getting to like you, getting to hope you like me. Getting to know you, putting it my way, but nicely, you are precisely, my cup of tea."* This song depicts teachers learning from their children. The outcome of this learning is captured in the words: "Haven't you noticed suddenly I'm bright and breezy because of all the beautiful and new things I'm learning about you day by day?" The implication of the song is that as we learn about others our days become more meaningful.

In some sense, people, even those caught up in day-to-day living are just faces until we actually get to know them. Getting to know them, getting to know about them, involves more than just a biographical sketch of the whys and wherefores of their lives.

When the Apostle Paul wrote about love he concluded his description of love with the words, "when I was a child my speech, feeling and thinking were all those of a child; now that I am a man [a grown person] I have no more use of childish ways. What we see now is like a dim image in a mirror; then we shall see face-to-face. What I know now is only partial; then it will be complete – as complete as God's knowledge of me."

Real, deep and abiding knowing of another comes from the face-to-face encounters of life. These happen when we take time to visit with each other. I say "each other" because I can't know you until you share yourself with me and I share myself with you. This calls for much honesty and trust. Honesty is the result of trust. Why? Because I hope I will be honest with you -- that is, share my deeper and more evident self. Yes, I am willing to be vulnerable when I think that you will be patient and kind, long-suffering and gentle with me.

This relationship is distant for most people, even within the confines of a marriage or extended family setting. Maybe we can approach the edge of such knowing by dealing with others in a caring and accepting way. We are able to do this by getting out of ourselves, so we can listen with caring ears and respond with a gentle tongue. When this happens, we have put away childish ways and become adults as we think of other before ourselves.

Another's World

MARCH 24, 2010

About a month ago, I wrote an article about what is going on in the lives of those around us. I posed the question, "Do you ever imagine what is going on in the world of those around you ~ those who pass you on the street, push the shopping cart in the grocery store, and serve you across the counter at the bank?"

Several weeks ago, I made my regular visit to the pharmacy. The lady across the counter has served me for a number of years. She is a middle age lady who works two jobs; that's all I knew about her. She has been helpful and exceedingly pleasant. I noticed that she had lost weight. I said to her, "You've lost some weight!" "Yes" was her reply. I then said, "Not easy to do!" [Since I have been trying to lose a few pounds, this was a natural response.] She then commented, "No not when your husband has committed suicide."

"I'm sorry!"

"And particularly when he killed himself in my presence." I asked if she had any children to which she mentioned a 30-year old son by a previous marriage.

I concluded my remarks with "You look good." With a smile on the face that had just shared a profoundly painful happening, there came the simple words, "Thank you."

I have been chatting with this lady for several years and exchanging humorous responses. Today was different. Such an in-depth disclosure of oneself is unusual. But I imagine the pain has been so significant, so very much on the surface that this was inevitable. Since then and forever more, she will not just be the person behind the counter fetching my medicine. She will be a person who carries a heavy burden and trying to find her way into a new day.

I hesitated to write about this situation. It is my hope that by doing so, I will encourage you, the reader, to look with fresh eyes upon the people around you. We all, myself included, are living and breathing and walking stories of sorrows and joys. One of the most profound teachings we learn from Jesus is "Blessed are the merciful for they shall receive mercy." This means that when we are able to get into the skin of others, and not only understand them, but show sensitivity, our life will be enriched. The Apostle Paul wrote the Galatians that they should think of others before themselves; in so doing, they would have the mind of Jesus Christ.

"The entire world is a stage, and all the men and women merely players." [Shakespeare] We are not merely players on the stage of life; we are people who carry great joys and sorrows, realized along our human journey. The challenge we all have is to see each other with reverence and care as together we take this human journey.

My Support System

MARCH 31, 2010

I learned last week that Super D has been bought by Walgreens. For the last umpteen years, I have been buying drugs from Super D. I have built up a friendly relationship with the druggists and support staff in the store. Now, I will have to start all over to identify and build relationships. I liked the way things were and the relationships I had. I don't want to start again, but I will. I will miss these folks who have taken care of me over the years.

Our life is a process of creating relationships and places that are familiar and comfortable. We don't like forming new relationships upon which we are dependent for our established routines and needs; we feel comfortable with the old ones. We don't like changing places. The same relationships and places provide continuity. With continuity there comes security. In other words, let's admit it, we don't like change.

It's been said that "change is the only aspect of life that we can count on." Seasons change. People change. Families change. Social structures change. And the list goes on and on. Possibly, the main thing is to learn how to deal with change. Even with change there is a certain continuity and regularity. The process of aging influences most of the change that is a natural part of our existence. This process shapes our individual and family life. The change in seasons provides a repetitive stability. The changes brought about by the discoveries of science and the developments of industry are built on an underlying emergence of discovery and truth. When we come to grips with this full reality of creation we are blessed with stability … the stability of a process within the ordering of creation.

Yet beyond this stability of the process we are told that our "help is in the name of the Lord who made heaven and earth." We find such words in holy writ that while earth and heaven may pass away, God will never pass away. God is alpha and omega, the beginning and end; he is from everlasting to everlasting. The Apostle Paul writes encouraging words to the Roman Christians that "nothing can separate us from the love of God in Christ Jesus … neither death nor life, angels or heavenly rulers or powers, neither the present or the future, neither the world above or the world below …" [Rom. 8:38ff] Take a stroll through the Psalms and you will find repeated references to the recognition of God's abiding providential care.

Hopefully, this recognition of an abiding God will empower us and assist us to accept the changes around us and to us. I believe that with this acceptance, we become more than conquerors through Christ who loves us.

Playing it Cool

JUNE 23, 2010

How often do we react to something another person may say? Family members, friends or just casual acquaintances may say some things with which we don't agree. On many occasions, the point of disagreement may be of little significance in the "grand scheme of things" -- not to mention the casual give-and-take of life. As years succeed to years, we gain insights that make the passage of time with others tolerable if not good. Maybe the perception that I am referring to here is "there are times when we should just button our lips;

yes, keep our mouth shut.

In the give-and-take of conversations, people say things that contradict what we say. In most cases, they are not seeking to argue with us or challenge us. They are just giving their points of view. I remember a teaching film I used many years ago which was entitled, "The Eye of the Beholder." The message of the film was that different people bring different experiences to the way they view the happenings around them.

If we are going to live in the give and take of life, we need to learn that everybody does not take life in the same way. Even then, we unfortunately may take undue issue with another's point of view. Then you might say, "Why am I doing this, if I need to give them their freedom of expression?" Possibly, just possibly, you may have a defensive streak in you. You may think you are right as they challenge you with their different viewpoint. How important it is to get beyond personalizing what others say to us. In the great scheme of life, there may be circumstances where "to our own self we need to be true." But always remember there are times to respond boldly and times to quietly listen. The point in life when we are able to do this comes when we feel real good about ourselves and never have to defend ourselves.

Let me take you a step further as we play it cool. Believe it or not, we can learn something from others. Their perspective may have value to us. I think real wisdom is expressed when we realize we don't know it all, and we can learn from others. Maybe with buttoned lips and open ears and a receptive mind we can enter other worlds of thinking. I often quote Nelson Rockefeller, a national figure of the last century. Mr. Rockefeller said that when we discuss something, the outcome may not be my way or your way, but a way beyond both ways; in other words, a more excellent way. Possibly somewhere beyond our words there may be that word of truth that will bring a ray of light to show us the way.

An added word to believers in a spiritual dimension brings us to the realization that the greater way of which Mr. Rockefeller speaks is "God's way": not my way or your way, but God's way. We come to that realization when we recognize that Jesus is at our table -- for through Him, we live and move and have our being. We should be at Jesus' table as he seeks to lead us by His word and the Spirit.

My Rights

JUNE 30, 2010

This coming weekend, we will be celebrating the 4th of July, our Independence Day as a nation. This is the day when the word "freedom" has sounded forth in print and word, with bells ringing and bands parading. This cry of freedom must never be muted -- for to do so is to allow the raging waters of personal gain to move with all of its slush and debris over the human scene.

We hear this cry today, loudly and clearly from the lips of the great human diversity of this nation. While the words from the multitudes are different, there is that single notion surfacing, spelled with the words "my rights." The founding documents of this nation have such words as "all men have been endowed by their creator with certain inalienable rights of life, liberty and the pursuit of happiness." This quote has often concerned me. On one hand, I believe that God has created all of us with these rights. On the other hand, if I persist in gaining my rights, there is the need to be careful that I don't infringe on the rights of others. There is a careful balance needed. Maybe the thought we need to muse over is "all men." As I pursue what is right for me, I need to realize that the differences which often cause inequality should melt away like a block of ice on a hot summer day.

The challenge before us comes in realizing what our religious freedom truly means. Celebrating the 4th on a Sunday moves us to recognize that in Christ, humankind has been set free from sin and death. It is the sin that claims our life in selfish gain. It is death that creates the clouds of fear and despair. Selfish gain, fear and despair are the demons of the day and night that possess our lives and cause denial of the rights of others, even when we are seeking our own rights.

I am drawn toward the Apostle Paul's words "to think of other before you think of yourself." When we do this, we do not count equality with God a thing to be grasped. When we are only concerned with our own rights, we have a tendency to count equality with God a thing to be grasped. More than likely, when we are pursuing the rights of others, not just our own, we will realize more fully the rights of all. Jesus said, "You can gain the whole world and lose your soul; but if you deny yourself, you will gain life."

Let Freedom Ring

JULY 7, 2010

Last Sunday, the Oakland Presbyterian Church announced the start of worship with the ringing of its bell. Nestled behind the church building is a pretty impressive bell. Our aim is to ring it every Sunday to announce worship, but this does not always happen. Last Sunday was a special day, Independence Day -- a particularly appropriate time to ring the bell. One of the cherished moments of my life was when my wife and I viewed the bell in Philadelphia that announced our nation's independence. A few brief words about this bell set the 4th of July in its proper context.

"Tradition tells of a chime that changed the world on July 8, 1776, with the Liberty Bell ringing out from the tower of Independence Hall, summoning the citizens of Philadelphia to hear the first public reading of the Declaration of Independence by Colonel John Nixon.

The Pennsylvania Assembly ordered the Bell in 1751 to com-memorate the 50-year anniversary of William Penn's 1701 Charter of Privileges, Pennsylvania's first Constitution. It speaks of the rights and freedoms valued by people the world over. Particularly forward think-ing were Penn's ideas on religious freedom, his liberal stance on Native American rights, and his inclusion of citizens in enacting laws.

The Liberty Bell gained iconic importance when abolitionists in their efforts to put an end to slavery throughout America adopted it as a symbol.

As the bell was created to commemorate the golden jubilee of Penn's Charter, the quotation, "Proclaim Liberty throughout all the land unto all the inhabitants thereof," from Leviticus 25:10, was particularly ap-propriate. For the line in the Bible immediately preceding "proclaim liberty" is, "And ye shall hallow the fiftieth year." What better way to pay homage to Penn and hallow the 50th year than with a bell pro-claiming liberty?"

The words on the Statue of Liberty give thoughtful clarity to the foundation of this nation. *"Give me your tired, your poor, your huddled masses yearning to breathe free, The wretched refuse of your teeming shore. Send these, the homeless, tempest-tossed to me, I lift my lamp beside the golden door!"* The ringing of the bell is an appropriate way to announce with clarity what this nation should be all about; yes, freedom. The resounding note needs to be the clarion sound expressed in Samuel Smith's hymn, "My Country 'Tis of Thee": "Let music swell the breeze; And ring from all the trees; sweet freedom's song.

Too often, we think of freedom as the result of a battle won and an enemy destroyed. A Christian nation should allow Christ, the Lord of Life, give us guidance where war shall be no more and the power of selfless love replaces the power of the sword. "Let freedom ring."

What you Can Afford

AUGUST 25, 2010

I was in a Collierville hardware store last week. As I prepared to pay for the item I bought, there was another person standing beside me. I said to him, "Have you gotten all you needed?" He responded, "All I can afford." His purchase was like mine; it was a single item you can only buy at the old style hardware stores. It was not necessarily an expensive item, so his response was a bit interesting. My thought was: this answer has a point.

Just think that if we followed the notion that we purchased only "all we can afford" what different lives we would have ... what a different nation we would have. Much of the economic difficulties where homes and jobs are lost are because of the human tendency to buy "more than we can afford." If we buy only what we can afford, we might not have as much. Our homes might not be quite as large. But our lives would be more stable. We would operate with much less anxiety. There would be much more harmony in our families and contentment in our hearts.

There is a song I sing in church, "When we walk with the Lord in the light of his word what a glory he sheds on our way." These take us along an interesting path. The insatiable thirst for more and quest for much more has infected our society. We build stately mansions for ourselves and temples of grandeur to God. And often, we can't afford them. But even more disappointing, we are disregarding the words of the Lord regarding the things of this world. Jesus said "Do not be anxious about your food, clothing and shelter. God will take care of you." Another says, "Don't lay up treasures on earth where moth and rust consume, thieves break in and steal; but lay up for yourself treasures in heaven. Seek first the kingdom of God and his righteousness; and all these things will be added unto you." "You can gain the whole world and lose your soul" and "Deny yourself, take up your cross and follow me" are others.

The Apostle Paul wrote words to the Ephesians: "quit stealing and work to meet your own needs where you can extend a hand of help to others." Could Paul be giving us some good advice? First, instead of operating on the premise of what we want, we operate more on what we need. Second, instead of simply working to meet our own needs, we also work to extend a helping hand to others. Maybe when we buy only what we can afford, we will have something left over to afford to help another.

Goofed

I Goofed! Have you ever said this about something you've done? Have you ever done something wrong and said, "I blew it!" Several days ago while blowing off my patio, I noticed where I had mended the extension cord in two places. It brought to mind why the mending was necessary. On two separate occasions while cutting the hedges, I accidentally cut the cord. You would have thought that I learned the first time to be more careful, but I didn't. Hopefully, the next time has been enough to avoid another such occasion. Regardless, once or twice, to make the extension cord usable, I had to fix it.

Mistakes, wrongdoings, goofs -- call it what you may, are all part of the landscape of our daily activities. We not only do such with inanimate things, but we do such with people. We can leave what we have done in the damaged condition or repair the item or relationship.

Repairing takes time and may be extremely easy or quite complicated; for example, repairing an extension cord. This repair job took some time, but was fairly straight forward. Once repaired, I was able to use it again. Had I left it broken, so to speak, it would have been of no use and I would have had to buy another. Some things can't be repaired and require replacing.

What might we learn from my experience with the extension cord? I was not paying sufficient attention to what I was doing; hence, a damaged cord. Giving attention to whatever we are doing (or with whomever we're involved) can save us much hassle and wasted time, and prevent irreparable harm.

Let's move to apply these thoughts to our relationships. The Apostle Paul wrote to one of the churches in the first century, "Think of others before you think of yourself." Often, the price we experience in human relations comes when we are preoccupied with ourselves. We fail to look beyond our own needs or interests to the needs and interests of others. Take time to pay attention to what you are doing. *It's a lot easier to keep the car on the road than it is to return to the road once you have gotten off.*

Empathy

OCTOBER 13, 2010

How can you win the battle of interpersonal engagement? Why do you call it a battle, Sam? I call it a battle because it often turns into a battle. We react to something a person has said to us and then they respond with a reaction. And the interaction sometimes spirals out of control. Each person is standing on their side of the line, defending. Before we realize it, the original issue of concern has been removed from the conversation, and we are in a battle to defend our personal integrity.

One of the greatest achievements in life happens when we reach the point where we don't pop off when someone else has said something we don't like. The further question that all of us are asking, "How in the world do you ever reach that point in life?" I guess to begin with, it takes a considerable amount of self-awareness and self confidence. Living life in our own little fishbowl and thinking what is being said is directed at us is often the culprit. It takes a quantum leap to turn away from being the center of the world, where everything is interpreted in terms of ourselves, to understanding the world of others. Better relationships occur as a result of such a change. But it can be done!

The Apostle Paul wrote to Christians in the first century, "Think of others before you think of yourself." The ability to do this is called empathy. The word "empathy" means getting out of your own skin and into the skin of another and trying to understand them. What are they saying? What are they feeling? What are they actually thinking? In order to do this, you have to get out of your own skin. When we are able to enter another's world, sensitivity and care take over. Openness is established. And using a familiar term, networking happens.

A dynamic and effective life is built around trusting relationships. We can't have trusting relationships if we chose to stay on our own island, seeking only to protect our place. It is when we are willing to venture off of our island into the other person's world that we expand our horizons of living. This takes a certain amount of self confidence and sense of adventure.

On the Road Again

OCTOBER 20, 2010

When you read this article, I will be "On the Road Again." I will be in Hue City, Vietnam. This is part of an 11-day tour of Vietnam from Hanoi to the southern part of the country. Someone said to me, "I believe I could find a better way to spend my money." My response was, "We all have our interests and usually spend our money on those interests."

For most reading this article, Vietnam conjures up a war in which the United States was most directly involved. The notion was that we were doing this to defend our nation from the spread of Communism. We saw repeatedly on television during the 50s and 60s soldiers from the United States and Vietnam dying. We would say the United States soldiers were dying to defend our country from Communism. On their side, they would say the Vietnamese were dying to defend their country from invaders. Times don't change very much. Over the last decade and continuing even today, people are dying, both soldiers and civilians, because for some reason we need to defend our country; today, it is the radical Muslims who are threatening us.

Wars, regardless of who is involved, bring destruction and death. I always wonder is it really worth it. There has to be a better way. I am reminded of the words of a spiritual song, "I am going to lay down my sword and shield down by the riverside and will study war no more." There is nothing I can imagine good about war, except in the case of World War II when a maniac had mesmerized a nation of people to believe they were superior and should rule the world.

Let me return to my reason for traveling to Vietnam or other places of like interest. Someone said to me who has travelled much: "You will come home realizing how well off we are in the United States." My response was "no, not really." While such a thought crossed my mind; I came back realizing how much 99 percent of the people in the world live their daily lives with a level of enjoyment and appreciation for the life they have.

Returning Home

NOVEMBER 10, 2010

One of the last times I wrote, I was going to Vietnam. I am home again ... hopefully with a little more knowledge about the world and a little wiser about life. Sometimes, I hear that to be different is to be strange ... to be different is to be uncomfortable ... to be different is to be inferior. The people of Vietnam surely are different from us. While different, the people of Vietnam are much like us.

We know that their form of government is different. But let me take you to a farming village. I wish I could share with you pictures from my walk through the living and working areas of this village. This farming village raised vegetables. One might say that the basics of a Vietnamese diet are vegetables. There were no tractors or combines or large acres of single crops. These were what we might call small family farms. The acreage was small. There were hoes instead of large cultivators. These hoes guided by a person were pulled by oxen. Instead of large sprinkler systems throwing water over large areas, there was a woman carrying watering pots at the end of a pole across her shoulders. The water was drawn from a well on the plot of land which might be equivalent to several acres. Instead of individual ownership of many acres of farmland, these few acres had been leased to the farmer for twenty years by the government. The houses were owned by each farming family. They were located within a community of homes within walking distance of their land. These homes were passed on from generation to generation.

Their homes were nice and were recently built. This farming community represents a manifestation of a nation on the grow. I would not want you to believe that all is well. There are many, many people living in extremely crowded areas in the cities ... with limited income. Even now, there is building and activity.

Let me share one more phenomenon found all over the country. Instead of automobiles crowding the streets and highways and even school parking lots, there are motor bikes swarming about like ants and bikes ridden by young and old. It was fascinating to find a people able to get about with much ease without an abundance of automobiles. By the way, driver's licenses are not issued until the age of eighteen.

A way of life so different and yet a people busy about daily living just like us. They had smiles on their faces and a gracious response to our presence.

Being an Example

JANUARY 19, 2011

Last Saturday a week ago, a nine year old girl, Christina, was killed by a young man. This girl was bright and engaged in life. She was born on a tragic day, September 11, 2001; she died as part of a terribly tragic act. The young man unloaded a number of bullets on a political gathering in a shopping area. He killed six people and wounded many more. This was a mentally ill person who had lost clarity of awareness about life. This event has occurred in the national arena of political unrest.

President Obama concluded his message at the community memorial service in Tucson, Arizona with a reflection that posed the thought that he would like his actions to demonstrate to the Christians of the world what is most noble and good. In saying this, the president was challenging all of us adults to reflect on what we do and say in light of our examples to children. As he spoke these words, a question passed over my mind: what a better world this would be if we, the adults of the world, in our acting and speaking would do so with the question in mind, "What example am I showing to children?"

I have often said that we, the adults, are the problem. We grow out of childhood, go through adolescence and into adulthood. Too often, that change erupts like a volcano. The ashes of personal gain and survival spread over the landscape. We have a tendency to become the center of humanity in our own minds, looking out for ourselves, rather than a part of humanity where we live in mutual care.

My Lord, Jesus Christ, said to his disciples when they wanted to push the children to the side, "Suffer the little ones; let them come unto me. And forbid them not, for of such is the kingdom of God." The faith of a child, expressed in trusting acceptance, is the focus of Jesus' thoughts here. Remember, when Jesus fed the five thousand; the child in faith gave all that he had to Jesus. Whereas, the disciple wanted to send the people home because of their lack of faith. Jesus responded by expressing thanks to God for the child's gift of fish and loaves; even more the child's faith. What we, as adults, may need to do is turn away from our self-centered ways, and in humility give all that we have so that the love of God manifest in Jesus Christ will empower us to manifest to our children all that are good and true and just.

United ... Divided

FEBRUARY 2, 2011

We find ourselves to be living in a world divided. We may even be part of these divided worlds within this world: families, divorced or dysfunctional ... neighborhoods formed in compounds ... children attending school because of personal preferences ... churches, bearing the name Christians, flying their flags under different banners ... nations at war with each other ... political parties pushing their own position The list goes on and on.

Isn't this what America is all about? Isn't this a place where we can exercise our individual rights; yes, do our own thing as long as we don't hurt others? We talk about states' rights as well as individual rights. This nation has become strong because of the ability to pursue our individual dreams and goals. But it has also become a vibrant nation because we not only live for our own rights but the rights of others. Even with the strong sense of individualism there is also a sense of community that enables us to build and share in a way that enhances all.

We may need to reacquaint ourselves with the phrase, "United we stand, Divided we fall." This phrase has been used in mottos from nations and states to songs. The basic concept is that unless the people are united, it is easy to destroy them. This is a counter to the maxim, divide and rule. This phrase has been attributed to Aesop, both directly in his fable, The Four Oxen and the Tiger, and indirectly from The Bundle of Sticks. The first attributed use in modern times is to John Dickinson in his revolutionary war song The Liberty Song. In the song, first published in the *Boston Gazette* in July 1768, he wrote: "Then join hand in hand, brave Americans all! By uniting, we stand, by dividing we fall!" This was also said by George Washington at the time of the start of the Constitution [From Wikipedia].

It is true that "unless a people are united, it is easy to destroy them." The lack of a sense of unity grows out of too strong an emphasis on personal rights. We position ourselves as if we are the whole rather than part of the whole. Individuals have made significant contributions to the progress of civilization; individuals have also caused much grief. But when we work together, we are able to enrich life for the multitudes and not just our individual self. We live in a multi-religious society, but I believe that the words of Micah [in the Old Testament] if followed would enable the sunshine of unity to enrich the whole wide-world. *"The Lord has told us what is good: to do what is just; to show kindness; to live in humble fellowship with God."*

A Thing

FEBRUARY 9, 2011

I had a unusually sad happening in my house last week. I broke something that was invaluable to me -- a porcelain eagle: it was a limited edition bought over ten years ago. I am a collector of eagles [wood, porcelain, metal, etc] This was one of my more treasured collectable items. Since I have been writing for the newspaper these last years, I tend to look for happenings in my life that can provide a notion of value. Martin Buber, a Jewish philosopher, wrote "We have a tendency to love things and use people. We must remember to love people and use things."

This eagle was a valuable and important item in my life. But when it broke into many pieces, I had to remind myself that it was but a thing which sat on a shelf. It was of aesthetic value, sure; but not something that required an extended period of grief. Being at the doorstep of eighty years, I have accumulated many things that are valuable to me, such as a library of books that brought the extended world of thought and life to me, a collection of crosses from other places near and far as gifts from family and friends, a collection of eagles, the furniture that fills the space in the house that is our home, not to mention the television and the computer inventions of the last seventy years that bring much pleasure and insight.

The other day, I had been watching the results of one of the many natural devastations where a fire had destroyed a home. I thought to myself, "how would I deal with such a loss?" The person being interviewed seemed to take the attitude, "the Lord gives, the Lord takes away; blessed be the name of the Lord." She went on to say, "We will rebuild." I imagine that this lady would heed the words of Jesus when he said, "Do not lay up for yourselves treasures on earth where moths and rust destroy, where thieves break in and steal; but lay up for yourselves treasures in heaven. First, seek the kingdom of God and his righteousness and all these things will be provided for you."

What really matters are not the things we have accumulated but our abiding relationship with God and our enduring relationships with others.

Getting Over It

MARCH 2, 2011

"There are things I do that I should not do; and things I do not do that I should do." These are words written by the Apostle Paul to a church he had established. We are reminded from these words how difficult it becomes to do the right thing or to avoid doing the wrong thing. The difficulty is manifest in habitual behavior and actions that become destructive to us. This habitual behavior often takes on the label of addiction. As we certainly understand, addictions describe habits over which people have little control and are found to be personally destructive. I think a few references, such as alcoholism, smoking, sexual indulgences, and preoccupation with material things might help improve our focus, but not limit the presence of others forms of addiction.

Words from a theologian of the last century come to mind. Paul Tillich wrote, "What is most important to a person is his or her god." The thing or person or activity in our life upon which we focus our thoughts and actions controls our life. Apart from the living and true God controlling our life, everything else doesn't always bring a helpful outcome. The above-mentioned addictions are concentrating mainly on ourselves [our personal ambitions or self-centered desires]. The more we are possessed by our own pain or pleasure, the more enslaved we are to relieve the pain or pursue the pleasure. As one might say, the focus is on "me, myself and I." People become the means to our personal ends and the world becomes our personal playground, rather than the people being the objects of our care and the world the arena becoming a place for expressions of goodness.

The Apostle Paul would describe this situation as a "body of death." Whatever obsession or vice or addiction we have puts us on the path of destruction -- with the ultimate outcome being the death of our soul or even our body!

Paul writes, "Who will deliver me from this body of death! Thanks are to God who gives me the victory through Christ." I believe that we can describe Christ as not only the third person of the Trinity, but also his healing and redeeming energy of life that issue from him. He moves us away from ourselves and hence our addictions or vices or obsessions to a close walk with God. With this close walk with God, we find healing and newness of life. I believe Christ is Lord. Therefore, we find His healing presence not only within the symbols of the church, but also the healing disciplines outside of the traditional church.

The Social Animal

MARCH 16, 2011

David Brooks has written a book entitled, *The Social Animal*. This title fascinates me. I have long believed that the emphasis on individual rights can be overstated. We are truly social animals and realize our full existence as the result of interaction with others. In a review of this book, I found these words: "It's not hard to see why this book about the human need for connection, friendship, and love speaks to the current social situation." Behind the elaborate theorizing is Brooks' desire to articulate a universal feeling: that all of us are caught up in what he calls "the loneliness loop." We yearn for community and we have "the urge to merge." When two people have an intense conversation, their breathing synchronizes; laughing together creates a sense of joy; soldiers drilling in unison experience a surge of power. What drives us, ultimately, is the need to be understood by others." And I might also add, "What completes us is our ability to understand others."

When we are focused too much on "me, myself and I," we fail to learn very much about ourselves. Jesus Christ spent much time talking about our responsibility to others and not being too preoccupied with ourselves. The Apostle Paul in writing to the many churches he established placed a strong emphasis on giving consideration to the needs of others, even before our own. A strong emphasis on individual rights often causes us to overlook a concern for others. We often talk past each other until we hear what pleases us. When we are so prone to seek after our own interests, we often fail to extend a helping hand.

Ultimately, I think it can be considered a matter of enlightened self-interest. What do I mean? A concern for others as we express a concern for ourselves will be beneficial to all parties involved, not to mention, in the thoughts of David Brooks, we need social interaction to achieve our own personal identity and destiny. Let's not listen with ears to hear what we only want to hear. Let's not engage in life's drama merely to work for our own benefit. Let's find a reality greater than what we can gain only for ourselves. Let's engage in a community of mutuality where we will realize the eternal dimension to life.

Have I Told You Lately

MAY 11, 2011

Have you told someone lately that you love them or care for them or appreciate what they have done? Van Morrison wrote a song entitled "Have I Told You Lately" The first verse of the song reads, "Have I told you lately that I love you ... Have I told you there's no one else above you ... Fill my heart with gladness ... take away all my sadness ... Ease my troubles. That's what you do." Affirming another person's value is a rich and rewarding act. It enables individual and relational life. It is the best gift you can give a person -- believe it or not, far more valuable than a precious diamond.

Last week, my wife took a cutting from a plant she has in our garden room to a recently established friend. This person had been in our home and commented about the plant. Becky, my wife, took two cuttings, one in a little pot and the other in a jar of water. I drove to the friend's house with Becky. When Becky gave it to her, there was a delightful and receptive smile on the friend's face and a genuinely delightful response of "thank you."

After we had gotten home, later that evening, I said to Becky, "You really like to share with others." She responded, "I do!" I thought it was important to acknowledge this neat quality in my wife. She is spontaneous in her giving; her giving ways are a significant part of who she is. It is part of her DNA. It is who she is! I believe it meant a lot to her for me to speak those few words, "You really like to share with others."

We can learn much from people who are spontaneous in their giving. A familiar saying comes to mind: "It is more blessed to give than to receive." These are words that Jesus used. The thought was also a common notion before Jesus in the life of the Jewish people. One of the scripture translations reads, "There is more happiness in giving than in receiving."

Maybe, maybe not! Think about times when we receive and exchange gifts. The focus is often on the gifts we receive, rather than the giving of gifts. Just think if you were part of a group of people and everyone received a gift, except you. You gave gifts, but no one gave you a gift. That would be a hard one to take, and yet "it is more blessed to give than receive." As I said earlier, "it takes a certain DNA" to be a genuine giver.

When you are giving, you offer something of value to another person. You give of yourself, your care, your love. What happens is you become a conduit of love. When the love of God genuinely passes through you in gift-giving, there is enrichment to your life. This enrichment comes from the joy of bringing a blessing to another's life as well as your own sense of personal fulfillment.

We have just celebrated Mother's Day. I would like to give tribute to MOTHERS, for in motherhood we find the most manifest expression of, "It is more blessed to give than to receive."

Near Death

JUNE 1, 2011

This probably will be my last article in the *Fayette Falcon*. I have retired from the Oakland Presbyterian Church and will no longer have any direct ties with Fayette County. I live in Collierville, Tenn. with my wife. My daughter and son and their children live in Collierville also. Before I leave you, I want to share my personal near-death experience.

I retired from full time ministry May 1997. The day I retired, I fainted and was admitted to the hospital for testing. I was supposed to preach in a Memphis church several days hence. This was delayed for a week. This unusual interlude in my life was to continue. On a Saturday night, I remember I was scheduled to preach the next Sunday. I felt like I was losing consciousness, and I was. Within a short time, I felt separated from my body and spoke out to my wife, "Becky call 911!" Fortunately, she did because the next minutes were claimed with much uncertainty. I felt conscious but out of it. My wife told me that one of the paramedics said, "We almost lost him!" With continued attention by the paramedics and the doctors upon my arrival at the emergency room, I again became a part of the fully conscious world.

What does an experience like this mean? I'm sure, different things to different people. But for me, a gift of renewed living. I could have seen this as a gift of new life for living out my life in meaningful days for myself. But I remembered words from my Mother's lips when I was quite young. "Sam, God has a plan and purpose for your life." So I began to think with this new breath of life, what is God's plan for my life? I could live for myself, or I could live with the mind of my Lord, Jesus Christ, for others!

We often hear people say upon retirement, "Now I can do what I want to do for myself." But a song kept echoing in my mind, "Living for Jesus a life that is true; bearing allegiance in all that I do." I believe when we live for the Lord, he calls us out of ourselves in the lives of others, inviting us be people for justice, bringing hope to the hopeless. As long as we turn away from ourselves in love toward others, we will share in God's life giving presence. May God's blessings be with you.

4. Acknowledge A Holy/Eternal Presence

Is there a spiritual reality beyond the realm of the human spirit that shapes an eternal dimension to our individual and mutual existence? For a long time, the evolution of thought throughout the earth's societies has moved to accept the concept of an expanding universe, beyond the moon and the stars, the outer galaxies. Humankind has from the beginning of recorded time lived with the belief in a divine reality -- a reality both as part of and outside of human existence in the physical realm. We make this reference by using a variety of words, usually translated with the word God. My wife and I have travelled throughout much of the world. We have found the repeated presence of religious activities that indicate a widespread belief in a spiritual reality. This gives further evidence that humans across the far reaches of the world are mutually engaged in the life-giving realm of the Eternal.

As I reviewed the articles for this book, I found numerous references to God. This caused me to recognize again that the reality of God is significant in my thought process. I have often quoted St. Augustine (3rd century) and Paul Tillich (20th century) in identifying the awareness of this reality. "Our hearts are restless until they find their rest in God." (Augustine) "Man [woman] has an ontological need for God." (Tillich) As I used occurrences and events to write these articles, I expressed an awareness of God. I recognize the importance of certain celebrations to remind people of God's presence. This presupposes God's everlasting presence. Finally, because of this consciousness, I have projected an attitude toward God in definite rather than abstract terms. All of this has led me to realize the need to acknowledge and express a holy/eternal presence if we are going to live under a banner of hope realized.

I, too, have learned from these articles that make reference to God that my awareness of God has been expressed with a certain hope. The times of our lives play out with blessings and hardships. How we interpret these occurrences is vital. A dynamic awareness of God as a Holy/Eternal Presence provides strength and direction for daily living, endurance in the face of uncertainty, and thanksgiving for blessings. The world is the field of God's renewing and sustaining presence. We then are able to express spontaneously with words learned as a child, "God is great, God is good, Let us thank him …"

Our attitude toward life has much to do with how we respond to the events around us. And our attitude toward God as a holy/eternal presence, makes a significant difference. From the articles, I have learned much about my own attitude toward God. We take charge of life when we stop trashing life and give God the praise. I recognize the core of my existence in words that describe the essence of God; it is more blessed to give (love) than to receive.

I would like to provide my reasoning for entitling this chapter, "Acknowledge A Holy/Eternal Presence." In the Christian faith, we recognize this presence in the words of the Gospel of John, "The (creative) Word became flesh and dwelt among us full of grace and glory." (John 1:1) In learning the children's catechism when I was a young boy, there was the question, "Who is God?" The answer was: "God is a spirit and has not a body like man." In this age of cybernetics, we can think of all life as being interconnected in an expanding field of energy. When I think of God as a spirit who has not a body like man, my thoughts move toward an eternal presence who embraces this expanded field of energy. Our very existence is realized as we are engaged in this expanding field.

So I am drawn to think about this eternal presence beyond time and space as being all in all; this eternal presence is in us and beyond us. I have chosen to use the word "holy" to describe the nature and activity of this presence as being set apart from and yet engaged with us as being "just and right and true." These words capture the context of hope realized; namely, life in a community where others are affirmed and personal selfhood is realized.

Ganges River, India

A *sunrise* is the *blessed* sign of *hope realized*. Our *life* migrates progressively out of *sunsets* into *sunrises*. The *Holy/Eternal Presence* calls us out of the *darkness* of our human *walk* into the *light* of the *holy ways* of the *right* and *true* and *just*. SBL

Hawaii

"*Water* is essential to *life* and a *blessed* sign of *eternal life*. A *dynamic* awareness of *God* as a *Holy/Eternal* presence provides *strength* and *direction* for daily *living*, *endurance* in the face of *uncertainty*, and *thanksgiving* for *blessings*." SBL

How Great the Pain

APRIL 8, 2008

It was Christmas Eve, in the evening! The door bell rang. I opened the door, and Rhonda, a young adult from the church I served many years ago, was standing there. She was crying and before I could say a word, the words, "Brent has killed himself" came rolling from her lips. Brent was her brother and several years younger. He was in high school.

Brent had been to camp the summer before. He had met a young woman with whom he had fallen in love. Through the Fall months, they corresponded quite regularly. Just before Christmas, the letter he received from her contained the words, "Brent, I don't love you anymore; I have found someone else whom I have been seeing." The outcome of these words brought Brent to the point of no return where he shot himself. He was found with a note, "Mother and Dad, please forgive me; I just didn't have anything to live for."

Why would a young man take his life? He did have so much to live for! He was part of a good family who loved him very much. He had his whole life before him. My son was a friend of Brent's. My son said to my wife and me, "I am mad with Brent. Why would he do this to his parents?" "Why? Why? Why?" becomes the resounding expression on the lips of all of us.

For whatever logical reason might be shaped for Brent taking his life, one might say the bottom line was that he found himself in such pain over his personal loss that the only way he thought he could relieve that pain was to take his life. I'm sure that we might find this hard to imagine ~ but believe me, a person can be in such severe pain [physical or psychological] that it becomes unbearable. The irrational takes control of life and death seems to be the only answer.

Many questions are asked when a person takes his or her life. Yes, God does forgive. God is a great God, and greatly to be praised. His greatness is measured in his unconditional love, not just his mighty power to create. Words of forgiveness I have used from time to time, capture the essence of God's love. *"As far as the East is from the West, so far has God removed our transgressions from us."* Nothing is outside the scope of God's forgiveness, God's grace. Please remember this! Press on! Claim tomorrow!

The Good

JULY 16, 2008

I asked my granddaughter the other day, "How are you doing?" The response I got was "Good!" I should have expected the response, because repeatedly in the past when I have asked most children the question, how are you doing? The answer I have gotten is "Good." I don't remember giving such a response when I was a child well over half a century ago. I wonder how this rather intriguing word emerged into the vernacular of the children's world. It is not a bad word to use. Actually, it is a profoundly <u>good</u> word to use.

When using the word, well, my mind gravitates toward the creation story in the Bible. In this story which describes how the world came into being, the word GOOD is placed on the lips of God when God looked back and reflected on the creation. It is written that God created the world in six days [perhaps periods of time]. The seventh day, he rested, reflected on what had been accomplished and said it is <u>good</u>.

I went to the Thesaurus on the internet to expand the <u>meaning of good</u>. The words I found were excellent, worthy, enjoyable, accomplished, beneficial, and fine. God in the creation story could have used any of these words to describe what had been accomplished. We are told that when we die we will have a "house not made with hands eternal in the heavens." Well this terra firma created by God is nothing to sneeze about ... not to mention the human body in all of its magnificence.

I am thankful every day that God has created me and given me the opportunity to live on this terra firma and engage in the give-and-take of personal life. There is a downside, but most of the time [99.9% of the time] it is fun to be alive. I must always be reminded that God created us, yes, you and me, to be caretakers of this terra firma; yes, and our bodies also, not to mention each other. The significant outcome of accepting our role as caretakers is "we all, every last one of us, benefit."

There is much being said these days about the sustaining care of the earth, the skies and the seas, the land and the lakes, the cities and towns and the people who dwell therein. Maybe we would do this with more excitement if we look at this creation as a little bit of heaven and why not, for we are told that the Spirit of the living God brought all of "this" into being. We have been blessed out of God's loving heart with this wonderful privilege to breathe the air and walk on the land, to laugh and be sad with each other. Yes, it is appropriate to say with God and our grandchildren, "It is good!"

Fear of Not Being

AUGUST 27, 2008

My mother had just tucked me in for the night. As I succumbed to those moments before falling asleep, a fear gripped me. At the young age of nine the thought of dying overcame me. My thoughts centered on the notion that some day I would die and never be again. I was being gripped with the fear of not being.

I ran down the stairs – our bedrooms were on the second floor. The refrigerator was kept in a little nook just outside of the kitchen.

There was just enough space between the refrigerator and the wall that I could comfortably nest. My parents were in the kitchen talking. They probably were thinking about getting ready to retire for the night. My mother saw me and called out, "What is the matter, Sam?" I responded, "I am afraid of never being some day." She took me in her arms with comforting words, "You don't have to worry, God loves you and will take care of you."

From time to time throughout my life, I have been gripped with what I call "this sense of non-being." And when such has occurred in my mind, it has often been when I have been extremely tired. This surge of fear will then swell up in my conscious mind and I ask myself, "What is it that causes such to happen?" Is it a lack of faith? I don't believe so. I truly believe that "I have been set free from the control of sin and death. I also believe I have received the gift of eternal life. I am also of the opinion that a person can have this profound belief in Christ, yet find herself [or himself] from time to time immobilized by this "fear of non-being."

Such a fear will [and had] cause a person to utter the words of Jesus' disciple –doubting Thomas, when he said, "I believe, help my unbelief." The sinking moments in our life when doubt and despair might grip us become reminders that we realize our ultimate destiny when we "walk with the Lord in the light of his way" night and day, in the good times and not so good times.

I believe that Jesus demonstrated such a touch of the fear of non-being. He cried out on the cross, "My God, my God, why have you forsaken me?" He then died. But before he died, he gave a sigh, yes, a sigh of peace that comes from a sense of God abiding presence. As I enter the last quarter of my first century of living, I approach this time with immense joy. I have come to accept this fear of non-being for I also know that God [in Christ] is alive and real. I know that God is at work within me to will and to do his good pleasure. I have a growing sense of the abiding presence of God.

So I press on to my high calling in Christ with the assurance that the "best is yet to be." The God who has given me life is the God who will sustain my life. The God of yesterday is the God of tomorrow. And this God is "the God who so loved the world that he gave his only begotten Son, that whoever believe in him will not perish but have everlasting life. I am assured that he did not come into the world to condemn the world, but to save the world." [John 3:16]

God is Everywhere

NOVEMBER 19, 2008

"The entire world is a stage and all the men and women merely players." I don't know what William Shakespeare fully meant in these words. The word "merely" throws me. Why? Because, I don't believe that we are just merely players. I have often said that life is much like ocean waves touching the shore line. The waves change the shore line. Our lives are impacted by the interaction we have with people and places. I am not bringing you a travel log of my journey to China, Cambodia and Thailand, but rather a glimpse into what happened to me as I took this journey.

Throughout my adult life, I have tried to think theologically about my journeys. Someone asked me, "Did you find Christians in China?" Of course, this would be a normal question when we think of China as a Communist nation. My response was that I found Christ in China. The presence of Christ was not only in people who bore the name Christian. My Lord's presence was found in the happiness and kindness of the people. His presence was expressed in the smiles and evident joy. I would be foolish to believe that these people do not have many of the dysfunctional problems we face in the United States.

I believe that God is sovereign over all of life. Furthermore, I agree with Paul Tillich, a theologian of the last century, that "we have an ontological need for God." We live and move and have our being in God. If we believe that God is everywhere and that the essence of God is found in all that is good and right and true, then "every time we hear a newborn baby cry or touch a leaf or see the sky, we know why we believe." This is true in China, as well as in the United States; it is as true in the smile and kindness of a person of Buddhist faith as well as person of Christian faith.

The noble themes of happiness, peace and harmony were part of the landmarks of their tradition and expressions of their lives. These themes are part of the core of who we are as Americans. One might say, there is not a whole lot of difference between us and them. We are mutually bound by the essence of life. I call this essence God, Alpha and Omega, the beginning and the end: my beginning and my end, your beginning and your end. Yes, in God all of us, live and move and have our being.

Noon Prayers

JANUARY 28, 2009

Last Wednesday, I started noon prayers for the community. Once a month I am providing for the extended community the opportunity to gather with me in a time of prayer. We live in trying and fear-filled times! The instability of the economy has brought uncertainty and insecurity for many of us. We need a shot in the arm to give us strength for the living of these days. In other words, we need some spiritual reinforcement. We don't have to fall off the wagon and tumble onto the side of the road; we can continue with confidence along our life's journey.

Because I am a believer in Jesus Christ as my Lord and Savior, I look to him for guidance in dealing with the give-and-take of life. There are four books of good news written about the life and teachings of Jesus; these books are called the Gospels. The gospel of Mark shows a prayerful pattern to Jesus' life. He had a demanding mission to accomplish. With each step he took, with each word he spoke, with each response he made to the demands placed upon him, his spiritual and physical energy was regularly depleted. Where did he go to be renewed? He lived by those familiar words, "In God I live and move and have my being." He had a pattern of life that involved regular prayer. He would go apart from his engaging life and spend time with God; this is not to say that God was not always with him. These were focused times with God. Mark suggests that when he returned from his prayer time, he was energized and activated. He was able to deal with the world and respond to the needs of the people.

This model is vital for our daily living. We are truly spiritual persons. Our help also is in the "name of the Lord who made heaven and earth." It is in God that we live and move and have our being. It is from our God that we gain our strength and wisdom for the living of these days. I believe that God is sovereign over all humanity. Prayer is not restricted to just my neck of the woods, the Christian community. While I believe that Jesus is my way to eternal life, I also believe that whoever we are our prayers expand into the living ether of God's presence. These prayers return to us as the healing balm of God's renewing and sustaining love.

Personal and private prayer are tremendously beneficial. But my final word is that our community prayer time also has immense value. Jesus said, "Where two or three gather in my name I am present." The gathering of believers, *what'er their faith may be*, seeking God's spiritual presence is a gathering with our Lord present. Jesus is always an eternal participant in the drama of a people's engagement with God. Let us come together to gain spiritual strength and claim God's vision for a new day.

Putting on your Holy Glasses

FEBRUARY 11, 2009

You never know! You never know where God will take you! You never know what God is leading you to do! One of the exploratory exercises that have become an integral part of my life is asking the question, "How do I understand the working of God in this event in my life?"

We can describe our lives in black and white. Life is either this way or that way. There are no variations to how we see life. What we see is what we see. What we hear is what we hear. The problem with seeing life merely in black and white is that we come to life's happenings and sounds with our internal filters. There is our conscience, which is shaped by all sorts of influences over the years. There is our ego, which often drives us to want too much for ourselves. "There is" goes on and on to give shape and form to what we see and hear. Most of the time, we realize life is not just black and white; there are many variations on the themes that roll out before us.

Then we can describe life in technicolor. Life is a many splendored thing! Life is not strictly this or that, but it takes on many shades … variations in movement and color and music. When we look at life through the prism of the many, we are able to manage the dynamic of all that is happening around us with greater ease and much joy. Life becomes a many splendored thing. We are able to accept differences in thought and behavior all around us. We are less frustrated with what is happening and more congenial in our relationships.

There is value in both ways of approaching life. But ultimately for the height and breath and width and depth of life to enfold us, one might say that there is another way to look at life. And this way is through the "eyes of God … through the mind of God … through the heart of God." In other words, how do I see or experience God in this or that occurrence? Asking this question is like putting on "holy glasses" that change the way we see the landscape of our life!

My wife shared some insights on a Biblical passage in an email she received. Inadvertently in sending a set of notes to her friend, she struck another key and these notes went to some of her other friends. She received an email from one of the friends with these words: "I don't know if you intended to send this to me, but it was a blessing. I have had a long difficult day. Then, BANG, there's Becky ... or BANG there's God. Reading through it got my frustrated head back on straight. Isn't God truly amazing!"

We could have interpreted this [yes, as happenstance] but her friend saw it as the working of God in his life. Don't forget that God is an integral part of your human experience. When we are willing to recognize "God's presence", we find fresh meaning and energy for the living of these days. Put on your "holy glasses"!

Eyes ... Mind ... Heart of God

FEBRUARY 18, 2009

Last week, I wrote about putting on Holy Glasses. In that article, I made reference to the eyes ... the mind ... the heart of God. As I re-read last week's article, I thought of the question, "How do you know the eyes ... the mind ... and the heart of God?" Let me make an attempt to answer this question.

I am going to write about the essence of God. Does it just come to us as a revelation directly from God? Is it something that is passed on from one generation to another? Do we find it in written form as in the Bible or the Koran? Is it something we are told? One might say all of the above; but all of the above with some clarification.

I remember when I was working as a student chaplain in a mental hospital in Elgin, Illinois 50 years ago. There was a woman admitted who had killed her twin sons. She claimed that God had told her to do this. Our instincts tell us that this couldn't be. Of course, it couldn't because such an act runs contrary to all that is natural in us and is contrary to scripture and societal teachings. Deep within her there was a confusion of thoughts which drove her to this tragic action. There are many things that are attributed to God that really cannot be ascribed to the will of God. Our mind … our conscience … our emotions form the reservoir that holds who we are and how we respond to life. The contents of our human reservoir always need what I might call the purifying agent of God's Spirit to shape the way.

In a sense, I suggest that this purifying agent of God's Spirit keeps our "Holy Glasses" clean. May I suggest that the cleansing agent for me is Jesus Christ. A theologian [Karl Barth] of the last century wrote, "If you want to know God, you look to Jesus Christ; if you want to understand what God intends man to be, you look at Jesus Christ." As I read the Gospels in the Bible, the good news about Jesus, I begin to see with God's eyes and understand with God's mind and respond with God's heart. Another theologian shared these words: "understand the world with an open Bible and a word of prayer." The ultimate truths of God come when we "work out our faith in fear and trembling, knowing that God is in us to will and to do his good pleasure." When we are engaged in a holy walk with Jesus, the crowning notion to remember is we are able to put on Holy Glasses. "When I walk with the Lord in the light of his Word, what a glory he sheds on my way."

GPS

JUNE 24, 2009

Becky, my wife, bought me a portable GPS for a trip to Atlanta. As we know, the purpose of a GPS is to give directions on how to get from one place to another, near or far. This device is guided by a satellite.

We have all become familiar with such a device. There is a picture on the screen showing the road on which you are traveling, and a voice telling you when and where to turn. When you make the wrong turn, the voice redirects you where to go. When you follow the directions of the GPS, you most often get where you intend to go. This instrument virtually took us to our destination and brought us back home.

I used the GPS again last week to go to a meeting in Whitehaven. I got there with no trouble. On the return trip, the directions and voice proceeded to taken me in a slightly different direction. In my resistance to this change, I took the wrong turn. The voice told me to turn around as soon as possible. When I took heed and followed the voice's instructions, I found myself back on the proper roadway [as the voice said].

This experience has given me a decidedly modern way of sharing with you my thoughts about God's critical role in our life's journey. Two words ~ connection and communication ~ come to mind. By way of the GPS, I was connected to a satellite that images the roads on which I travelled. Within the system, there is a programmed voice that communicated with me and provided directions as I approached various intersections. This voice also gave me confidence that if I made a poor choice she would give me guidance on what to do.

I am not suggesting that our relationship with God is that automatic or simple; but it certainly can be that real. Reading the gospels, we learn of the close walk Jesus had with God: "I and the father are one." In the relationship between Jesus and God, there was communication and connection. He was one with God. He was clear in that what he shared with his disciples he had heard from God. He took much time in prayer. He knew that it was in the ways of God that he lived and moved and realized his destiny.

Comparing our relationship with God to the GPS can be particularly helpful. We can come to realize that what we cannot see can be real. We can have a relationship with life in the spirit. We can truly be connected to God and communicate with our God. Once we make the commitment to trust God, we can relax and know that there is assurance along the way. We are able to proceed along our journey of life with confidence.

Awareness of the Entire Scene

JULY 1, 2009

Life can be viewed up or down or all around! I have one more story in me from our trip to Chicago. There are two buildings in Chicago where the expanded landscape of the city can be viewed; these are the Hancock and Sears buildings. Our hotel was just around the corner from the Hancock Building. From the ninety-sixth floor, there is a magnificent view of the city. You are able to look out and see Lake Michigan and the far reaches of the city; one might say, "It was like an ant world in action."

I take a lot of pictures when on vacation. This is a way of documenting my trip. It also enhances my recollection of the happenings around me. Among the many buildings, most relatively high, along Michigan Avenue there is an isolated building, The Tower. This building is not noticeably large or high. I took a picture of it at ground level, then another from the ninety-sixty floor of the Hancock building. On the ground level, it had some dimension and proportion to the space around it. From the top of the Hancock building, it became insignificant.

What do we gain from this reference? When we are observing life on the ground floor of human interaction, we have one view on reality. When we look at life from a distance, we often get a more expansive picture of the human scene. One might suggest that the closer we are to each other and the events of our time, the more difficult it is to discern the totality of life. And our failure to discern the totality often prevents us from responding accurately or truthfully.

I want to associate engaging life at the street level to seeing things from a human perspective. Viewing the landscape from a high building is like seeing things from a divine perspective. Reality is put into its proper perspective on the top of the high building. Jesus' invitation to engage us is an invitation to go to the top of the high building and see life with holy glasses, as God sees the world.

I am reminded of the words of the Apostle Paul when he wrote, "When I was a child I spoke and acted as a child; I look through a glass darkly. But when I became an adult, I put away childish ways. I come to know God as God knows me. Now abides faith, hope and love, but the greatest of these is love." Going to the top of the building is like loving as God loves: seeing and living life in touch with reality and out of the heart of truth.

Persistence

JULY 22, 2009

The distinction of being steadfast despite problems or difficulties is captured in words such as perseverance, determination, doggedness, diligence, resoluteness. All of these words imply a goal, something toward which a person is moving or reaching. One might say, "And nothing, no – nothing, is going to get in the way of achieving my desired outcome."

"Nothing, no - nothing" is a bold statement. When I probe further into the implications of this statement, there needs to be some clarification. I don't mean you should not have regard for other people in your persistence. The truly modifying factor in a persistent life is a significant regard for others. Jesus, my Lord, was a persistent person when it came to being faithful to God and his calling. We remember that he gave his life so that others might have life. He challenged others in their narrow thinking and self-centered ways. Even as he challenged, he did so in love.

Jesus believes that [in the words of a familiar hymn] "this is our Father's world and though the wrong seems oft so strong, God is the ruler yet." In order to remain persistent for the good, we have to believe the good will win over the bad, right over wrong, truth over falsehood, justice over injustice. With such awareness, we come to realize "nothing can separate us from the love of God." Persistence, more often than not, is grounded in the belief in a greater power. As one might say, "come hell or high water" we press on.

I believe that one of the significant components in life is claiming something of value either for oneself or beyond oneself and doggedly pursuing it. Great personal accomplishments come from being resolute and diligent. Major discoveries have been the result of persistent exploration. Significant changes in the fabric of society for justice have happened because people have claimed the truth and doggedly pursued it even in the face of personal danger.

In order for "persistence" to shape your journey, you have to believe with your whole heart, claim it with your whole soul and engage it with your whole being. You can't give up because of the obstacles, the momentary failures, or the discouragement of others. You have to keep on keeping on. And don't "be dismayed what'er betide, God will take care of you."

Sin ~ Learn More About Me

AUGUST 12, 2009

Last week, I referred to sin as "doing and living contrary to the law of God." Have you ever referred to sin as a disease? There is a variety of ways we can define "a disease". Let me take the definition as this one: "a disorder in humans, animals, or plants with recognizable signs and often having a known cause." Let's use this definition for sin. Sin is a disorder in the psyche of humans with recognized signs and often having a known cause.

We have been created "in the image of God to do the will of God." Sin then is defined as denying our creation in the image of God and not doing the will of God. Of course, when we do this, we are placing ourselves at the center of our lives rather than God. It is like having a party and only inviting "me, myself and I" to the party. It is like having worship and placing our picture at the center.

In this context, the recognized signs for sin are pride and despair. Both of these words describe a person where God is absent. Such a person is sick to the heart, soul and mind.

A companion word to pride is arrogance. The prideful person has heart, soul, and mind centered on himself. He lives his life for his own pleasures. He set goals for his own benefit. He utilizes all of his resources for the realization of his own personally defined game plan. The way he deals with people and the world around him is determined by his own set of principles. There may be some compassion in all he does, but ultimately, it is to enhance himself.

Then there is despair. This is when we are all tuckered out, beat down to a pulp and think we have nowhere to turn. We end up in the ditch of self-pity. We don't even feel forsaken by God because we don't believe God can help us. On the one hand, in pride we are engaged in self-aggrandizement; on the other hand, in despair we are engaged in self-pity.

The Apostle John wrote, "all have sinned and fallen short of the glory of God." In some way or another, we all have thrust God from the center of our life. In some way or other, this disease grips us all. The Apostle Paul wrote, "Who will deliver me from this body of death." "Thanks be to God who gives me the victory in Christ" was his answer. King David found himself imprisoned by pride and despair. He asked for God's forgiveness and cried out to God for a new heart so that he might give praise to God and extend love and justice to others. The wonder about the God we reject is that he is the same God who accepts us even though we have sinned. "How Great is God!"

Learning through Suffering

OCTOBER 21, 2009

This last Sunday, a significant part of the scripture reading were the words: "In the days of his flesh, Jesus offered up prayers and supplications with loud cries and tears to the one who was able to save him from death, and _he was heard because of his reverent submission. Although he was a Son, he learned obedience through what he suffered_; and having been made perfect, he became the source of eternal salvation for all who obey him." [Hebrews 5:7-9] The words that I have underlined have three words that I used as the focus of the sermon. These words are faithfulness, servanthood and suffering. I want to replay the basic thoughts that each of these words suggest.

There are so many objects of faithfulness we could reference, namely, family, self, country, and the list would be endless. But most of all, for us to realize the fullness of "who we are and what we are about," faithfulness to God is essential. "We have been made in the image of God, to do the will of God. [Brief Statement of Belief, 1963] St. Augustine wrote, "Our hearts are restless until they find their rest in God." Let's just assume that the restlessness that drives us to reach for exceptional heights for our personal fulfillment is a misguided search for perfection. Let's just assume that this restlessness is actually a genuine need for communion with God. Then the journey we need to be on in life is not the quest for success, power and recognition, but the journey into the mind and heart of God. In God, we live and move and realize our being and that over time becomes more clear to us.

The second word I pursued was servanthood. Two of Jesus' disciples tried to get Jesus to give to them places of honorable standing on his left and right sides. This caused much dissention in the ranks of all the disciples. Jesus responded by saying, "but whoever wishes to become great among you must be your servant, and whoever wishes to be first among you must be slave of all. For the Son of Man came not to be served but to serve, and to give his life a ransom for many." [Mark 10:44, 45] The destructive ways of humanity emerge when we seek equality with God. In so doing, we often diminish the value of those around us. The way of true humanity comes when we work in mutual love and care with those around us and "think of others before we consider ourselves."

The last word is suffering. Part of Jesus' redeeming act was his suffering. No one wants to suffer. We do so much to avoid it. Yet because of the dysfunctional conditions [physical, spiritual, social] suffering happens. The important thing to learn is "suffering is not our enemy; it can be the springboard to a deeper and richer life." Suffering can become the transformative agent in our life where we are able to say, "I have become a better person because of my suffering."

God in Action

NOVEMBER 25, 2009

This week, I went to the hospital to visit a member of my congregation. I had to park in the parking building, a fair distance from the hospital. I'm sure you can connect with this experience. Usually, I would have to climb several levels before finding a place. On this day, I entered the building and moved closer to where I would have to turn to another level and move further away from the ramp to the hospital; this meant a longer walk. I often rationalize with myself by thinking that the longer walk is an exercise opportunity. As I approached that turning point, a car was pulling out to leave. A space close to the ramp became available.

I was going to say "a space was provided." This would imply that someone or a reality beyond space and time made this space available. When I was in theological seminary, I had a professor who truly believed that when he arrived at the downtown square, the Lord would provide him a place to park. He would drive around the square several times when he did not find a place. A place would become available. He believed this was God's doing. We all thought that this was a little much.

God is "working his purpose out as years succeed to years." But I still think it is a little much to think exactly the same way as did my professor. I do believe that in the providence of God that God is working for the good of his creation, even down to you and me. The Apostle John wrote that "God so loved the world that he gave his only Son, that whoever believes in him will not perish, but have everlasting life. He came not into the world to condemn the world, but to save the world." (John 3:16). I learned this verse when I was a child and these words have become words of much assurance. God is intimately involved in our life.

It is not inappropriate to see such an experience that I had in the parking building as a blessing. This is the season of recognized blessings. This is what "thanksgiving" is all about. Instead of seeing this as happenstance, why not allow oneself to believe in God's blessings in the give-and-take of the smallest and largest of happenings in life. Being able to park closer was a blessing. As you share in the bounty of God's creation this Thanksgiving, express your appreciation for God's abounding grace, overwhelming mercy and intimate presence from day to day.

The Gathering

DECEMBER 2, 2009

One of our members asked me after the Community Thanksgiving Service, "What are you going to write about in your article this coming week; I imagine it will be this service!" He went on to say, "This sure was nice [meaning the service]." The Tuesday before Thanksgiving in Oakland is becoming a tradition. This is the day we hold our community Thanksgiving service. The crowds are not overwhelming, but substantial. Most of all, the atmosphere was joyous, and the fellowship was excellent. We introduced the new-comer to the community, the pastor of the Faith United Methodist Church. The offering becomes a gift to Fayette Care, the principal organization that reaches out to the needy in the county. Someone commented, "We should have more of these community gatherings". One of the ministers commented that he looked forward to this community service.

Our congregation was excited about hosting this service. I mentioned in my welcome that the building in which we were worshipping was built in the late 1800s. As I look around Oakland, I imagine that this church building stands close to the tops of the list of the most historical. I have defined this church building as being at the crossroads of Oakland, and it is at the crossroads. So to gather at the crossroads is symbolically, if not actually, recognition of what community is all about! People come from east and west; they come from north and south. They assemble in this place of worship to give praise to God. Even more fittingly, our gathering expressed what the Christian faith is all about, "one in the Spirit, one in the Lord, and they'll know we are Christians by our love." Possibly, this gathering in worship can become a catalyst for a growing sense of community in Oakland – and elsewhere.

The major theme of the message was story-telling at the table of grace. I am going to take the liberty to share with you my reflections. Thanksgiving is a time when family members gather from here, there and yonder. When we are together, we share our stories, our memorable times as we bring each other up-to-date about the whys and wherefores of the past year. The thanksgiving table for us is a table of grace. Around this table as we share our blessings, we are reminded of God's abounding grace. This grace is manifest in bounty from creation, but also foremost, the new life of salvation given to all humankind in Jesus Christ. And with this expressed awareness we give thanksgiving to God for all of his goodness. Amen and Amen.

How do you Keep Hope Alive?

DECEMBER 16, 2009

As I mentioned last week, we are in the Advent Season leading up to Christmas. Christmas is the day we celebrate the fulfillment of the promise by God of a new day for people. The promise was "the suffering and despair of their current lives would pass and there would be a new day." With the anticipation of the new day, hope is real and alive. We express this in the words of one of the carols, "The hopes and fears of all the years are met in thee tonight." We are referring here to the coming of the Christ child.

I want to spend some time this week, and the next several weeks, on the question, "How do we keep hope alive?" "Keep hope alive" are the words for which Martin Luther King is remembered. President Obama has written a book titled, The Audacity of Hope. Sometimes, it is difficult to keep hope alive, so the title, The Audacity of Hope. Of course, the simplest way to keep hope alive is to see and experience positive signs that encourage us in our hopefulness. But when all around us seems to indicate doom and gloom, it is difficult to maintain the hopeful posture with raised head and deliberate steps, a strong spirit and encouraging words.

So how do we keep hope alive? Let's always remember that our hope for the good and just and true is established through our faith in God. When we further focus our sight on Jesus, the Christ, as the basis of our faith, then we have a firm basis for keeping hope alive. We focus on one who "took the form of a servant even to the death of the cross. He has been highly exalted where every knee will bow and tongue confesses that he is Lord." He intercedes for us, but not just for believers but all the peoples of the world, all God's children.

Often, we allow the destructiveness around us to shape our notions about life and when we do this, we lack any sense of a positive future. We allow ourselves to become weighed down with the worries of life. The outcome of such posturing is to choose a life where we eat, drink and are merry for we believe that tomorrow we will die. The tragedy of such a life is that we stop living, stop fighting -- merely exist and slide into a life of nothingness to dull the feelings of despair. So sad!

When Jesus entered on the human scene, the Hebrew people were weighed down. In so many words, Jesus encouraged them not to give up. It was essential to live in anticipation of the day of fulfillment. Jesus might have said to them, "I know that it is hard and difficult to be upbeat. Let me assure you that God is good and just and God will prevail. I have found that one significant way to keep my head up and my footsteps sure is to live in a prayerful relationship with God. So don't ever forget, the life God has announced and promised in Jesus Christ is not despair and hopelessness, but fulfillment and hope."

Merry Christmas and Happy New Year

DECEMBER 30, 2009

A friend in his usual manner said to me, "I have a question to ask you!" My response was, "If I am able, I will answer it." He then asked,

"Where do the expressions of Merry Christmas and Happy New Year come from?" Since I could not be specific with him, I suggested that he check the internet. When I got home, I went to the internet and typed in Merry Christmas and Happy New Year. I was able to find a reasonably declarative answer for Merry Christmas, but not Happy New Year. I would like to share what I found.

The term, merry, itself arouses in us the feelings of joy and happiness associated with the festival of Christmas. Though the Christmas celebration, as history tells us commenced from the 4th century AD, it was only in the year 1699 that the phrase Merry Christmas came to be used. An English admiral plays a significant role in the History of Merry Christmas. In 1699, he used the term Merry Christmas for the first time in an informal letter.

The words Merry Christmas appeared for the second time in 1843 in Charles Dickens', "A Christmas Carol". The term Merry Christmas is used to greet each other during the festival of Christmas by all, irrespective of class or religion. In the term Merry Christmas, 'Merry' stands for happiness while 'Christmas' meant Christ's Mass in old English.

Many people use the word happy instead of merry to wish each other during the festival of Christmas. The phrase Happy Christmas gained much popularity in the 19th century, as it was used by none other than Queen Elizabeth II. Its worldwide popularity is also evident from the fact that the concluding lines of Clement Moore's work, "A Visit from St Nicholas," written in 1823, which included the words Happy Christmas was changed to Merry Christmas in the various other editions of the book.

The term Happy Christmas is primarily used by the inhabitants of Ireland and United Kingdom. Sometimes to cut it short, many use the word Xmas instead of Christmas. The truth is that no other term or phrase can even wish to match the popularity of Merry Christmas.

Since I was unable to get a declarative answer for Happy New Year, I will suggest a few ideas. No doubt, we could extend the notion of merry standing for happiness to the New Year following the Christmas event. The coming of Jesus marked the beginning of a new age. This is described as bringing blessings to the whole of God's creation. Jesus delivered the Sermon on the Mount. In his words, we find pronouncements of blessings to the poor, the mourners, those treated unjustly. With such blessings there comes the touch of happiness. It is reasonable to say Happy New Year, for we are reminded that the God of all creation intends for all people to be blessed. Yes, Merry Christmas and Happy New Year!

An Angel and a Star

JANUARY 6, 2010

The last item to go on the tree at our home is the angel, placed right on top. Our granddaughters helped us decorate our tree. While one of the granddaughters was doing this last ritualistic act, I said to her, "Do you know what the angel points to or even the star?" [Some people put a star on the top of their tree, others put an angel.] She responded by saying, "No, what!" I went on to say, "The angel represents the coming of the angels to the shepherds. The star reminds us of the wise men."

She then asked me where I read this. I said to her that I had just thought it up. Several Sundays ago, I shared in the children's message at worship these thoughts about the star and the angels on the top of the tree. I called their attention to the decoration on the top of the tree in the sanctuary. It was a star. I mentioned to them that my family put an angel on the top of our tree. Then I asked for a show of hands from the congregation as to who had a star or an angel or nothing on the top of their tree. It was pretty equally divided between stars and angels. A few didn't have anything.

I have since been to the internet to explore my notion. It is clear that this notion was not original with me. Both the star and the angel are part of tree decorations. You can buy a treetop ornament that includes both the star and the angel.

The angels did announce to the shepherds at the birth of Jesus: "Peace on earth, goodwill to all men [and women.]." The star led the wise men, the sages from the east, to the manger of Jesus. They brought precious gifts to him. They allowed themselves to be led by the star which gives guidance to all people, rather than the limited ways of Herod, the ruler of that day. Christmas strikes the note which allows us to wish each other a Happy New Year. The angels and the star direct us away from the plains of human selfishness to the gift of a new day in the birth of Jesus, the Christ.

Today is Epiphany in the Christian Church. This is the day we celebrate the coming of the wise men. We are reminded that their wisdom came, not from man, but from God, the one who is sovereign over all humankind. Why not say to those near and far, Happy New Year *"for unto us a child is born, a son is given; and his name shall be called wonderful, counselor, son of God, prince of peace.... And of his kingdom there shall be no end."*

The Voice in the Storm

JANUARY 13, 2010

I am hooked watching movies on the western TV channel. As I sit down at my computer to write this article, I am watching "Southwest Passage." A surveyor looks through his scope across a plains area to a distant mountain. A person with him asked, "What do you see?" The surveyor responded "Take a look!" Looking through the scope, the person said, "A man holding a pole." The surveyor then said, "That's interesting; I see roads and cities." "I don't see that." "Well they are not out there now, but some day they will be." The person in a musing way said, "You won't benefit from it." "I will have the satisfaction that I have had a part in the development of these roads and cities."

This conversation reminds me of an educational film that I used many years ago. The title was "In the Eye of the Beholder". The essence of the film was that we see what we see and respond the way we do because of who we are. Every person is a composite of culture, experience and their own DNA. As a result, each of us sees life in a certain way. It is so valuable that we learn this if we are going to live together in our families, our hamlets or on the planet earth.

I read Psalm 29 yesterday in preparation for a prayer time at the church. The psalm is entitled "The Voice of the Lord in the Storm." The essential message is that with a storm, we hear God's voice and are aware of God's power. While there is much destruction as a result of the storm, God strengthens his people to deal with the storms of life. His ultimate intent for all the people of the world is peace.

As we begin a new year, according to the calendar, there are some basic thoughts that should give us assurance for the future. We live and move and have our being in a world that has been created by the voice of God. The powerful voice that we are aware of in the storm is the same voice that created order out of chaos and brought light out of darkness ... the same voice that affirmed Jesus as the "eternal word that became flesh and dwells among us, full of grace and glory." Karl Barth in the middle of the last century wrote "If you want to know what God is like, look to Jesus. If you want to know what God intends for man to be, look to Jesus." The words and actions of Jesus affirm over and over again his words, "My peace I leave with you, my peace I give to you, not as the world gives, do I give to you. Let not your hearts be troubled, neither let them be afraid." If we are going to be co-creators with God, we will never reach the peace that passes all understanding by the blade of the sword. We will reach it by seeking to live in mutual respect in a climate of justice ... aware of the voice of a powerful God of justice in the winds of the storm.

The Ability to Endure

FEBRUARY 24, 2010

Life is quite interesting! Every day, in larger or lesser ways, we have to stand up after being knocked down ... continue to persevere when there is strong resistance ... push on even in the face of uncertainties. We come to understand that great lives take shape in the crucible of difficulties. We find these words in the Bible: "My brothers [and sisters], consider yourselves fortunate when all kinds of trials come your way, for you know that when your faith succeeds in facing such trials, the result is the ability to endure. Make sure that your endurance carries you all the way without failing, so that you may be perfect and complete, lacking nothing." [James 1:2ff]

Last week, Christians all around the world began a period in the life of the church called the Lenten Season a time of fasting for some Christians. This is a forty day period of repentance and abstinence from certain nonessential things. From time to time, we need to come out of the world and recognize how much we falsely rely upon ourselves and the treasures of this world. We need to re-establish the truth of our ability to endure as "we walk with the Lord in the light of his word." When I find myself to be relying on "me, myself and I" then I know I am in trouble. But when I claim the realization that "my help is in the name of the Lord, who made heaven and earth," then I know this I have the ability to endure. I know I have overcome!

During Lent our attention is drawn to Jesus' 40 days in the wilderness. After receiving baptism for the repentance of sin and the anointing of the Holy Spirit, Jesus went into the wilderness. He first engaged in the act of abstinence [fasting]. In so doing, he was framing his ability to endure whatever tests he was to face. This would be done with the understanding that "we do not live by bread alone, but by every word that comes from the mouth of God." Fasting is not merely a ritual act; it is a way of reminding us, assuring us, that enduring the trials and tribulations of this life comes from a "close walk with God". Jesus was also tempted to give in to the human tendency to claim power over others and ownership of the things of this world. The temptations were met with a strong resistance and endurance because Jesus gave himself to God completely. We come to realize during this season of the church's year [if properly practiced] that endurance is not merely a matter of survival. Endurance is also a matter of overcoming the temptations we face daily by having these close walks with the Lord.

I am reminded of the words from a song "We shall overcome some day ... Oh, deep in my heart I do believe we shall overcome some day."

Forgiveness and Generosity

MARCH 3, 2010

This last week, I was watching the TV program on retired living. The woman being interviewed was asked to identify from her experiences with people the qualities she considered being most significant. Her response was quick and to the point: "Generosity and forgiveness." I was grabbed with her response -- not only what she said, but how she said it. I would like to spend some time with you in this article musing about the value of these two qualities. We might also explore what it takes to express generosity and forgiveness.

When we think of generosity, I imagine our first thoughts are in terms of money, yet we can just as easily talk about the generosity of time. Both involve the abundant giving of oneself. People have been helped. Schools and hospitals have been built. Lives have been saved. Yes, these have occurred because of the generosity of people. Such references lead us to the awareness that generosity involves the free and abundant giving of ourselves, our time and our material resources. Generosity involves something extremely basic to human nature, which is a concern for the well-being of others. This concern for others takes a bit of getting our own interests out of the way before we are able to respond to the needs and challenges of life around us.

But we have to admit that often there is a bit of self-interest. We are often motivated by a desire for personal recognition in our generous acts. *Regardless of whatever self-interests there may be, the giver will be happier and the world a better place to live.*

The other quality mentioned is forgiveness. Forgiveness does not hold another person's destructive ways against them. The forgiving person is not quick to judge or even quicker to exact punishment. When harmed, this person is not eager to employ retribution. <u>What does it take to</u> set <u>the desire to retaliate when an</u> offense <u>has been committed</u>? Again it takes forgetting oneself and genuinely being concerned for the well-being of another. *Instead of retaliation and retribution, restoration becomes the driving force; and the world becomes a better place to live.*

If we have been brought up in a Christian church, one Bible verse we learned is "For God so loved the world that he gave his only son that who ever believes in him shall have eternal life. For Jesus did not come into the world to condemn the world but to save the world." [John 3:16] Generosity and Forgiveness ~ the heart of God and the essence of life!

God's Presence

MARCH 17, 2010

I learned a catechism when I was a child. This was a little booklet with questions and answers about my faith. Some of the first questions included references to God. Who is God? "God is a spirit and has not a body like man." Where is God? "God is everywhere." This description of God was telling me that God was not some old man in the sky or some powerful cosmic being. I was being told God is like the air I breathe. I cannot see air or touch air; feel it, yes. Air is all around me and in me. In the same way, God is all around me and in me. When I start with this all-embracing aspect of God and not a superhuman description of God, I then begin to realize what it means to say, "I live and breathe and have my being in God."

Several Sundays ago, I preached the sermon using Psalm 63. The writer in this psalm identifies his experience and understanding of God in two main arenas of his life. The first arena is where he lives and moves and has his being in his daily activities. This activity was in the desert where the lack of water causes one to thirst. He writes about thirsting after God. As I read his words, I reflected on the thought that all of us experience reality in different settings. In whatever setting we find ourselves, that setting can help us describe God's reality in our life. Think about how the routine of your life defines you and in that discovery God can talk to you in a special way.

What happens to you when you enter a place of worship? Is it just a building where you participate in a variety of activities? Possibly, while you are there, you are grasped by the majesty and wonder of God. Caught up in that ethereal experience do you ever realize an elevation of spiritual presence? We don't only live and move and have our being as earthly creatures traveling horizontally. The reality of life is not altogether without the awareness of the spiritual dynamic all around us.

The last thought I want to leave with you is the importance of meditation or reflection. The psalmist would meditate or reflect on the presence of God in his life at night when he lay on his bed. Do you ever take time at night before you go to bed just to think or reflect? I'm talking about more than counting sheep. I'm talking about as we move about in the growing and caring aspects of our life we realize how God is engaged in our growth and encourages our caring. I'm also talking about when we are brought through the "shadows of despair" how we have found strength [from God] for the living of our days. Who is God? "God is a spirit and has not a body like man." Where is God? "God is everywhere."

An Intervention

JULY 21, 2010

The scripture which was read during last Sunday's worship was the story of two sisters. Mary and Martha lived in Bethany outside of Jerusalem. Jesus had raised their brother, Lazarus from the dead. Jesus was on his way to Jerusalem with his disciples. The group had stopped by their house for a meal. Martha was busy caring for the guests. Mary was sitting at the feet of Jesus, listening to words about his journey to Jerusalem. Martha was upset with Mary because she was not helping her with caring for the guests. Jesus responded by acknowledging the importance of Mary's listening. A valuable insight comes from this story.

There are many ways we can describe the activities of us humans in the day-to-day happenings of daily life. One we might liken to a bee hive. I'm sure you have heard the phrase "busy as a bee." From sunrise to sunset, we humans are busy at the work of keeping the wheels of society running, our own lives functioning. Visit a factory or farm or hospital or just walk the streets of a large city and the video you would take is one of people moving and doing. I imagine most of us feel comfortable with this lifestyle. All of us are caught up in what I would call "Martha living."

Unfortunately, life is not this way. Storms come, unexpected happenings occur, and comfortable routines are interrupted. When our human activities are the beginning and end of our understanding of life, we miss something. Martha in her responsible and caring manner, like most of us, missed something. I believe that "God is working his purpose as years succeed to years." And from time to time as he works his purpose out, God intervenes. An intervention is an intentional action to prevent a situation or change the course of an event, particularly when the situation or event seems to be going in the wrong direction. As Mary listened to Jesus, she was aware of God's intended action to bring new direction and new life to an evil world; it was a loving intervention. "For God so loved the world that he gave his only Son; that whoever believes in him will not perish, but have everlasting life." God continues to intervene to give us guidance and direction for the living of these days. An important question all of us need to ask is "Am I too caught up in my routine that I fail to recognize God's presence and hear God's special Word to me?"

Worry

OCTOBER 6, 2010

I began a weekly reading time this last week with one of the first grade classes in the Oakland Elementary School. What a delight it was to share with these well-behaved children. The story I read was about a little girl who had the habit of worry. She worried about everything. On her way to school her first day, all she could do was worry about the unknown world she would be facing.

You don't have to be a child to worry about the unfolding events before you or the various conditions and circumstances around you. Earlier this week, which will be last week for you the reader, I got up, ate my breakfast and got ready to go to the doctor. I thought I had gotten up in time to make the appointment. Well, a few events here and there delayed me and my margin of adequate time diminished. I still thought I would get to the doctor's office on time.

I had forgotten that along the way there were two school zones. A major section of the street I travelled was under construction. Well, as I continued along the way, I had to slow down through the school zones. When I reached the construction, I found myself in a long line of cars moving quite slowly. Anxiety began to creep in with the thought that I am going to be late; probably not too late, but late. I began to realize that I would be late and I said to myself, "Sam, you'll get there when you get there …you can't do anything about it. Stop worrying!"

When you think about it, worry does not solve the problem or improve the situation over which you are concerned. By worrying about being late, I would not get to the doctor's office any faster. The only thing is that worry only does harm to the human psyche. It makes you nervous and anxious and causes consequences hurtful to one's self and others.

I am reminded of the words of Jesus, "Don't be anxious about your food or clothing. Look at the birds of the air, they neither reap nor sow or gather into barns, but God takes care of them. Are you not as important, person of little faith. Seek first the kingdom of God and his righteousness, and these things will be provided for you." In other words, Jesus is saying to claim that inner peace God provides, slow your emotional motor down; yes, and be not dismayed what'er betide, God will take care of you."

Finding a Way
NOVEMBER 17, 2010

A time to behold! All that can happen will happen. Jesus brought a message of a new day. People had committed themselves to Jesus. It would be a new day. Not just a new day, but a new age would come after a dramatic change in the landscape. Nature would speak resoundingly with change and upheaval. The conflict of nations would take front stage. Centuries come and go and these words are as fresh as the morning dew. It seems that nothing much has changed on the stage of history. With the passing times, we are still players on the stage of history. "How do we play the game?" is the real question. Jesus' guiding words to his disciples may have some value for us today. Don't give in. Be aware of God's guiding presence. Endure.

Don't give in! The temptation in every age: people let society control their life. Some think it is easier that way. It surely will relieve the pain of outward persecution or the inward pain of struggling over what is right in the face of destructive social norms. Take the easy way! I am reminded of the words of Jesus that "You can gain the whole world and lose your soul. Take up your cross and follow me." Giving in will do this for you: a loss of integrity, self-esteem, and value. For this reason, Jesus taught us to pray, "Lead us not into temptation, but deliver us from evil for thine is the kingdom and the power and the glory forever. Amen"

Be aware of God's guiding presence. We often talk about God's protecting presence. This comes in the form of words from a hymn based on the Psalms, "Be not dismayed what'er betide, God will take care of you." God will take care of us. But he does not only as an objective reality in our life, but as a guiding presence. It is true that there are many voices, often different in content and direction, coming from the churches, political leaders and many others today. It is often not the loud voices but the quiet voices that give strength for the living of these days. So listen amidst the clapping thunder and the flashing lightening and the loud voices of people … listen for that still voice of God, particularly in the words of Jesus.

Endure! Last week, I had one of my usual periods of sleeplessness. While there, I watched a movie that told the story of a group of Australian women who were held in a camp by the Japanese during World War II. Some relented and made themselves available to the Japanese officers, but most of them continued to endure. Their conditions went from bad to worse. Many of them died. But together, they endured. Please note I said "together they endured." They encouraged and supported each other.

It is true that we can tell story after story of persons who have endured without the visible support of others. Even within this group there were individuals singled out to be punished harshly as an example to the group. They endured. But in the full scope of these ladies' time of trial, it was obvious that their strength came from each other. They were able to bear up under the long trial because of each other. In their words and actions, you could see they all were part of a greater energy field, their faith in God which sustained them. I am reminded of the words of Jesus, "Where two or more are gathered in my name, I am there." [paraphrase]

Prepare the Way

DECEMBER 15, 2010

A new day has begun … a new day has begun … there is no secret what God can do. What he has done for others he can do for you. These words from one of the gospel hymns communicate a note of joy. The time in which Jesus was born with all of its debilitating dimensions was on the verge of slipping like a landslide into the sea. God was bringing something new to into being. This something new was being focused on "Jesus, the Christ." "For unto us a child would be born, a son given … and he shall be called wonderful, counselor … the everlasting king … the prince of peace."

The people were being told that they should prepare the way for this new something for themselves and for the world – how? By the act of repentance, by turning away from their sins [simply stated from a self-centered life to a God-centered life]. Sin can be described in terms of a variety of 'immoral acts' but the bottom line is that sin is living outside of the will of God which results in human destruction and a breakdown of society. We learn that you can even be in the church and quite religious and still be outside of the will of God. We are gripped with the words of the Apostle Paul "all have sinned and fallen short of the glory of God."

There is no way to accept the new that is happening on the horizon unless we are prepared – prepared to see, hear and to respond. If we are looking into the setting sun of the past, we can't see the rising sun of the future. If we are listening to the sounds that make us comfortable, we will not be able to accept the new sounds that resound with a fresh note, a noble hope and an uplifting joy.

Again we might ask the question: How do we prepare the way? We stop trashing life and living like we are in charge. We acknowledge we have been participating in a way of life that is not always ennobling to the God who has created us and continues to sustain us. We throw off those false securities to prepare for God's new embrace. We turn from our life in the world and fall prostrate on our face giving homage to God and stand up once again with a renewed sense of the Spirit of God empowering us and leading us.

The Measure of the Man

JANUARY 12, 2011

I suppose you have heard people use the phrase, "The Measure of the Man." In this day and time, we would more than likely say, "The Measure of the Person" which would include both women and men. We are referring in this phrase to the characteristics of a person that give her/him quality and value.

My son has two sons. I was in his house a while back and he pointed out a place where he periodically measured their height. In certain arenas, height and even weight would factor into the measure of a person for a place or position in life. In addition to the physical qualities, we often establish the measure of a person by what has been accomplished or accumulated. But what is the true measure of a person?

I am reminded of the words of Jesus where he said, "Don't be anxious about what you eat or drink or wear or your height. Look at the birds of the air, they neither reap or sow or gather into barns, yet God takes care of them. Seek first the kingdom of God; and all will be well." [Paraphrased] These words quickly move us toward a different level of discussion. We are invited to consider, if not to embrace, our relationship with the Eternal as the basis of the measure of a person. Remember the words of Jesus at the age of twelve in the temple. He said to his Mother, "I must be about my Father's business" [meaning God]. And when he became an adult he was baptized with the Holy Spirit with the words being spoken, "This is my beloved Son, in whom I am well pleased." He lived his life in the arenas of this relationship.

"We have a real need for God." [Paul Tillich] "Our hearts are restless until they find their rest in God." [Augustine] These words go to the heart of the matter; that is, "We have been created in the image of God to do the will of God." When we are able to live and move and realize our existence in the essence of God, we demonstrate the true "measure of the person." May I suggest, simply stated, God is love; a love so amazing so divine, demands my life, my all." Can I do anything more than "give of my best" for God so loved the world that he gave His best.

Happy!

JANUARY 26, 2011

It is always a delightful gift when I get a clear response to a sermon. I received an email this week which read, "Your sermon nailed it!" I responded by asking "What do you mean by nailed it?" The response came back, "When I feel like you're looking into my soul and pointing a finger right at ME, that's nailing it. You were saying (and not in these words) that if one were not happy, that the trouble was more with one's relationship with God than what is going on here on earth." Bingo! There are a lot of things I cannot change about my life, but I can improve my relationship with God.

Think about those times when you were happy: The birth of a child. Children doing well in school. Good job performance. A joyous family gathering. An enjoyable vacation. These few references along with many others you might think of can be described as giving you a sense of fulfillment and pleasure. Not only happenings but good relationships bring happiness. So it goes to say that we are unhappy when unpleasant or harmful things happen in our life or we find ourselves in dysfunctional relationships.

I believe the above quote is suggesting that we are not always able to shape the happenings around us and to us or control the response of other to us. But God is always consistent. Day in and day out, we can depend on God's everlasting love. And we do have a say about our relationship with God. Jesus, in the name of God, says, "Come unto me all who are heavy laden and I will give you rest." We are told that those who trust in the Lord will be happy. We will have a sense of contentment and well-being, regardless of what is happening around us and to us. Jesus said, "My peace I give to you, not as the world gives; let not your heart be troubled."

Let's not forget that we can trust God to take care of us. He gives us an inner sense of well-being that enables us to function in the face of changing times, uncertain events and disastrous happenings. So I would suggest it is important to "take time to be holy, speaking often with our Lord." I have a prayer bench from Libya with some thirty crosses from around the world hanging over it. The bench is there not only to remind me, but provide for me a time to be holy where I can speak to the Lord. The crosses are there to remind me of the abiding love God has for me and people. God's promise is that when we take time to be holy and trust in him, nothing can separate us from His abiding love.

My Father's World

Maltbie Babcock wrote a hymn at the turn of the last century [1901] entitled, "This Is My Father's World." The last verse of the hymn reads, "This is my Father's world, Oh, let me ne'er forget, that though the wrong seems oft so strong, God is the ruler yet. This is my Father's world: the battle is not done; Jesus who died shall be sanctified, and earth and heaven be won." With all that is going on in the world today, it is valuable to re-express these words. We could end up in a deep pit of despair if we were to let all that is happening at every level of life, in all corners of the earth control our daily thoughts. Yet, we also might wonder that "if God so loved the world and does not want to condemn the world" why there is so much upheaval, turmoil and bloodshed? I guess such a question deserves an answer!

The world scene [including happenings in our own country] places before us social conflicts resulting in bloodshed, natural disasters, and governmental conflicts. With the exception of earthquakes and floods, many of the other happenings are man-made, as one might say. "Most of the disasters of the world are made by men and can be solved by men." [President John F. Kennedy] And there is much truth to these words. Even the natural disasters that cause much upheaval and destruction can be solved by humankind. When the institutions of society such as the government and the church, are built around social concerns, the outcome can be renewal. Whenever there is a disaster, near or far, we see private agencies, governments and the churches mobilizing their resources to help … and of course individuals from all corners of the earth.

Since I have a tendency to think, as one might say "theologically," I would affirm, "Oh let me ne'er forget, that though the wrong seems oft so strong, God is the ruler yet." I have a tendency to pass up trying to answer the question, "Why does God allow this to happen?" When I think of Jesus proclaiming that the "Kingdom of God is at hand" I am caused to think beyond my own personal salvation to believe "God has got the whole world in his hands" and "He works his purpose out as years succeed to years." I know that someday I will die! And I believe that this planet earth more than likely will not last forever. But in the meantime, this is still "our Father's world." Between life and death, we and this world, belong to God ... the God who, having created the cosmos, continues to bring light out of darkness and order out of chaos. In the meantime, I guess I should work like everything depends of me, and pray like everything depends on God.

This is the Day

APRIL 6, 2011

"This is the day the Lord has made, let us rejoice and be glad in it." These words from the Bible have been rattling around in my head for the last week or so. Possibly, these words entered my consciousness when I heard someone say, "I think we should live each day with meaning and purpose as if it is the last day of my life." So often, we have a tendency to live each day anticipating the future and fail to enjoy the richness of the present.

"Today is a day that the Lord has made." I reflect on the words, "when God completed creation, on the last day, he rested. He spent time looking over his creation and saw that all was good." In other words, there was a sense of pleasure and completeness and well-being in the mind of God. We need to realize that God continues to work his purpose out as years succeed to years. The earth shall be full of the glory of God. There is so much to enjoy each day, as creation unfolds. The natural dynamic of life should bring immense pleasure and joy to our lives. The give-and-take of human life with all of the joys and tragedies, the interaction of people and the unexpected happenings give us so much for which to live. We lose so much of life's blessings when we just live with a little awareness of what is happening. The challenge is to come down out of the stands and participate in the game [of life].

Clara H. Scott wrote a hymn over one hundred years ago: "Open My Eyes, that I May See." The second verse begins with the words, "Open my ears .... " Both of these phrases continue with "glimpses/ voices of truth .... " Other phrases in the hymn are "place in my hand the wonderful key that shall unclasp and set me free" and "while the wave notes fall on my ear, everything false will disappear." These words remind us of the rich tapestry of life all around us.

We can go through life oblivious to what is happening around us. We become like the three monkeys, "no see, no hear, and no speak." We can stay at home within our predisposed world, or we can step outside see all that is happening around us. Even more, we can take a walk around the corner … or a trip to the next town with open eyes and ears. This may mean getting out of our present routine, whatever it may be, and opening different doors that will take us into different realms of doing and thinking. "This is the day the Lord has made, let us rejoice and be glad in it."

Epilogue

The title of this book, *Hope Realized*, inspires us to believe that our life's journey can have a positive outcome. We can claim a vision for our life and live with the hope that we can realize that vision. Such a belief enables us to endure the hardships and difficulties, overcome the hurdles and realize our purpose for living. Such a movement requires turning away from merely living for self-gain, affirming the holy/eternal presence and becoming a person of sensitivity toward others. Believe it can happen! Such a belief will keep us moving along the way. Let's remember that we must view and interact with the landscape with a sense of interconnected value. The world and those that dwell here do not exist for me, but we exist for each other in mutual support of our common journey through life.

This approach to life would call for a radical change in interpersonal relations such as family, society, government and even the church. This lifestyle calls for the shaping of a sane world while we are now living on the edge of insanity. We are driven today by an insatiable need for self-realization through an accumulation of things, an acknowledgment of self, and the exercise of power. The crucial question is, "How should we view and react to the landscape as we move along on our journey?"

The way we view and react to the landscape depends on how our inner eyes are focused. They need to be focused with an awareness of the opportunities, blessings and dynamic holy/eternal presence that empowers us. Let's face it, there is a proclivity in the human psyche where we do not see blessings as easily as we see the destructive factors operating in life. We find ourselves too often in the valley of despair, rather than on the clouds of high hopes. We have a greater tendency to criticize rather than to affirm. We miss the opportunities that open doors into a sane new world, because we are fixed on our individual moments of glory.

My son ran track in high school, the hurdles to be exact. There is a lesson to be learned from that athletic activity. This race is a wonder to watch; it takes timing and precision to move from one hurdle to the next and then to jump the hurdle without stumbling and falling. If the runner hits the hurdle and stumbles, he could either give up or lift up his body and move on to the next hurdle to finish the race. Running the hurdles requires endurance. Our lives are similar to this as we move along the way and view the landscape.

There is much to learn from what we see and hear along the way, but we have to keep our eyes on where we are going. We can't let what is happening distract us from the race we have chosen in life. Learn from hurtful events, but don't let them discourage you. Learn from successful events but don't let them restrict you. Too much of what is happening around us shapes our life and determines the way we run the race; we can be shapers of the landscape, rather than being shaped by the landscape.

As we move forward to realize our purpose, we need a clear understanding of our past. We have a proclivity to embellish the rich accomplishments of our past and moderate the destructive happenings. For example, I have observed there is a certain blindness as we look back on the history of this nation. We tend to diminish all of the destructive factors that have brought us to this time in history: the dehumanization of other humans, the abuse of creation, the engagement of our adversaries with destructive force, just to mention several aspects of our journey. The way we view the past has a definite influence on how we will move into the future.

As I have studied these many articles and viewed the landscape on my journey, it has become clear to me that we need to examine the way we approach life. There seems to be a form of individualism that is like cancer, eating away at the actualization of community and the possibility for purposeful life for all people; both are necessary for the full realization of the human species. I like to think of myself as a person living in community with other people. Together, we are on a journey to realize our special purposes; rather than individuals on a quest for our own "glory in the sun".

What are the hurdles we face as we run to reach our hopeful purpose? Maybe it is not a matter of listing the hurdles although they are present, as we will learn. It is a matter of looking at the techniques being used; in other words, not only how we see but also how we engage the landscape. There is a logjam today on the American stage in the way people engage each other. This is manifest in two major institutions: the government and the church. Both of these institutions play a significant role in shaping the lives of the people.

The most profound evidence of the problem is in government. Each political party is aligned around a set of principles that are in juxtaposition to each other. One set of principles stresses individual achievements with the accumulation of possessions and establishment of position as primary. The other party focuses on persons living and working together in community where there is mutual assistance in caring for each other. One set of principles does not necessarily stand in a superior position to the other. One emphasizes a strong individual. The other affirms the importance of a strong community.

The necessary note to strike is that both principles have value; the value of each is diminished when chosen to stand alone. A dynamic interplay between these principles is needed in the search for a direction. We might say "you can't have one without the other." Or we can say, "We are mutually dependent on each other if we are going to reach our individual aspirations with integrity." I am reminded of a quote by Nelson Rockefeller: "The outcome of a creative discussion that is seeking a solution is not necessarily a compromise between the two ideas, but rather is a new insight that has been created by the discussion of the different positions." [Paraphrase]

In government, unless people in the different political parties are willing to show respect for each other, nothing will be accomplished.

There needs to be that mutual belief that the people in both parties [as in any personal interaction] are of value and have something significant to contribute; and if either is incapable within the limits of their thinking to express this recognition, then very little will be accomplished and all the people will ultimately suffer, with too many perishing.

Christian churches also are infected with this disease of self-absorption. People in churches need to join hands and hearts under the banner of Jesus Christ's command to "deny self and take up the cross of sacrificial compassion as they follow Him." Unfortunately, the driving force behind the life of many churches is the damaging notion (we might say damning) "I am right, you are wrong" when it comes to a discussion where there are differences. In churches, there is the tendency to make absolute expressions of piety or purity. These absolutes unfortunately become the controlling factors rather than the unconditional love and profound sense of justice that Jesus expressed.

The proclivity to draw a line in the sand where our personal principles define what is absolute causes strife, dysfunction and division, be it in the church, government, the home or on the streets where humans interact (press flesh). I would like to dwell a little more on the dysfunction in the churches of this nation. There has been a loss of the full meaning of "church," namely, a people called by Jesus Christ out of the world to be a community of mercy and justice wrapped with unconditional love as they re-enter and participate in the world. A rank individualism is often expressed by the church in an excessive emphasis on personal salvation in those instances when there is blind neglect of also giving hope to people caught in the degradation and despair of human situations. The outcome has too often been building self-serving institutions rather self-giving communities. This is not Jesus' way! Church people need to be challenged to follow their Lord as they give not only their money and their time but themselves; in doing this, they truly identify with the forsaken and forgotten of the world.

There is an engine that runs much of the mindset of this society. This engine is "self-realization" by acquisition and acclaim with the exercise of individual power [to repeat myself]. The fuel that keeps this engine running can be described as a mixture of ambition and greed. Also, I have come to believe that the fear of death and the desperate desire for survival give shape to this malignant condition of life. Once we overcome this fear of death, we no longer have to fight with others for survival. We can begin building communities where joy and thanksgiving create the songs of life.

From the most precious relationship between grandparents and their grandchildren to the ones between public leaders, we are faced with the need for forming strong interactive relationships of mutual care and respect, not only to survive, but to realize life fully, for one and for all. Such relationships are essential for the building of community. A healthy community is the seedbed for growing people of character and vision. Our personal destinies are dependent on such relationships. Our lives together on this planet earth depends on such relationships. It may all come into focus when the well-being of others and our self-interests are engaged simultaneously; this is called "enlightened self-interest."

Yes, hope can be realized! Hope for a happier day, a fuller life, and a brighter tomorrow can be realized. Hope where every human being can stand on the mountain and view the landscape with a sense of well-being can be realized. We can even shout from the mountain, "Go tell it on the mountain, over the hills and everywhere, go tell it on the mountain" that hope can be realized. Such hope can be realized when we are willing to recognize our identity as we take up our cross of abiding care for each other.

I would like to conclude [as I began] with the words from Rabbi Ben Ezra by Robert Browning:

> "Grow old along with me, the best is yet to be;
> The last for which the first was meant."

The Final Word

My final word is a tribute to Jesus, the Christ. The Apostle Paul wrote to the Galatians, "It is no longer I who live, but Christ who lives in me." [Gal. 2:20] My editor, David Yawn, has shared with me several poems he has written. These poems are presented from a Christ-centered viewpoint. I have chosen to share one of the poems that captures the perspective of my book. This poem reminds me that Jesus, the Christ, has given meaning and direction to my journey. He has marked me with the importance of caring for others, even to the point of self-sacrifice, as the pathway to personal realization. He has turned my attention toward the oppressed and neglected. He has helped me reaffirm the importance of living together in love and justice. He has given me a sense of freedom from the sin of self-indulgence. He has provided me release from the fearful death of non-being. He has opened my eyes to the crippling danger of religious idolatry expressed in both piety and purity. He has harnessed within me this sense of hope in the present that enables me to claim the future with joyous anticipation. As you have read my book, I hope you have found the same hopeful claim on life and a renewed sense of your own journey that I have gained in writing it.

Day of the Lord

Far from city, county or state,
The kingdom comes for all who await.
A procession never ending --
A ruler never to abdicate.
Lead on, O King; reign with your own
At the city on a hill -- everywhere known.
A site whose light cannot be extinguished.
Not to be duplicated in any manner or way
Is this Holy City in its day.
Mighty in strength -- the King in majesty
Summons His people to listen to verity.

They willingly come in multitudes from
    every land --
For His words are their sole demand.
How long have we waited
To see the king manifest
And His own fully blessed.
As the new day dawns,
Tears give way to service redeemed
At the realization of millions of hopes
    and dreams.

By David McDonald Yawn; ysanctus@aol.com

Hawaii

"Don't you *know?* Haven't you *heard?* The *Lord* is the *Everlasting God;* He *created* all the *world.* He *never* grows *tired* or *weary.* No one *understands* His *thoughts.* He *strengthens* those who are *weary* and *tired.* Even those who are *young* grow *weak;* young *people* can fall *exhausted.* But those who *trust* in the *Lord* for *help* will find their *strength* renewed. They will *rise* on wings like *eagles;* they will *run* and not be *weary;* they will *walk* and not grow *weak."* Isaiah 40:29-31

Sam B. Laine

Sam Laine was born and grew up in New Orleans, La. He graduated from Tulane University in Chemical Engineering and worked for Pan Am Corp. for a time before serving in the U.S. Army for two years. He attended Columbia Theological Seminary, Decatur, Ga., graduating cum laude with a divinity degree. He studied at Austin Theological Seminary, Austin, Texas where he worked on a master's degree. He received his Doctor of Ministry from McCormick Theological Seminary, Chicago, Illinois. while serving as pastor of the Westminster Presbyterian Church, Lubbock, Texas.

By 2014 he will have been in the Presbyterian ministry 55 years; serving churches in Arkansas, Louisiana, Mississippi, and Texas. After retirement in 1997 and moving to Collierville, Tenn., he served as interim pastor of several churches in the area.

Throughout his ministry, he has played a significant role in civil rights and community service.

Sam has had the privilege of traveling throughout the world since his retirement. He has spent time in Great Britain, Europe, South Africa, Zambia, Egypt, Israel, China, India and Southeast Asia. In his travels in the United States he has visited Hawaii and Alaska. The appreciation he has gained for other cultures and religions has enriched his sense of the Holy/Eternal Presence.

He is married to Rebecca Laine and they have two children Sam H. Laine and Tamah Halfacre. He has enjoyed retirement watching his five grandchildren grow up close to him and Becky.

He tries to live his life from his core faith in Jesus Christ, the true model of unconditional love, and the words in "Rabbi Ben Ezra" by Robert Browning, "Grow old along with me, the best is yet to be; the last for which the first was meant." The logo that frames his life is "Future Grasp".

Index

2008

2009

2010

2011

INDEX